CURT

CURT

THE ALAN CURTIS STORY

ALAN CURTIS
WITH TIM JOHNSON
AND STUART SPRAKE

MAINSTREAM
PUBLISHING

EDINBURGH AND LONDON

First published in Great Britain in 2009 by
MAINSTREAM PUBLISHING COMPANY
(EDINBURGH) LTD
7 Albany Street
Edinburgh EH1 3UG

ISBN 9781845964924

A catalogue record for this book is available
from the British Library

Typeset in Caslon and Headline

Printed in Great Britain by
Clays Ltd, St Ives plc

For my mother and father

ACKNOWLEDGEMENTS

Friends and family have offered support, advice and encouragement in bringing this project to fruition. I would like to offer a big thank you to everyone concerned. To my co-author, Tim Johnson, who has ensured I have met the many deadlines along the way. To Alun Dodd and John Bowen: they have contributed enormously with ideas, proof-reading and analysis. To Phil Sumbler for allowing us to carry on his initial project. To Wyndham Evans and Leighton James for their memories of the Swans. Rosalind, Lucy, Emma and Josh have provided support throughout – thank you very much. Ian Parkhouse provided me with his expert knowledge of IT. To Liam Sullivan, John Walters and Gareth Vincent at the *South Wales Evening Post* for allowing us access to their archives, which proved invaluable. Thanks also to Alan, who has had many offers to have his story told but gave Tim and me the privilege of helping him to write his book. My special thanks are reserved for my late mother-in-law, Gwenllian Davies of Pwll. Without her support and encouragement over the years, I would not be where I am today, although she would not be best pleased that I am writing football books! *Diolch Mamgu*!

Stuart Sprake,
September 2009

Special thanks go to Sian for her love, support, patience and endless proof-reading skills. To Mum and Dad and the Johnsons Down Under! Also, to all the people who helped with advice and contributions to all aspects of the book. To Alun Dodd for his continued enthusiasm and thoughtful contributions, Martin Brown for his memories of Elland Road in 1979–80, Stuart Noss for his suggestions on the Saints chapter, Howard Evans for the background to what life was like in the Rhondda in the 1950s, and Sean and Michael Dwyer for their thoughts on the Bluebirds chapter. As promised, a mention to Lewis Haynes and the 'politics gangs' of 2008 and 2009. We would also like to thank everybody at Mainstream, especially Paul Murphy for his advice on editing the manuscript. To Stu, my co-author: big thanks for initially suggesting the project and for the hard work over the last 18 months. Finally, to Alan who's been a real gent and a pleasure to work with – thank you for sharing your story with us and for all the coffee.

Tim Johnson,
September 2009

CONTENTS

FOREWORD

The thing I remember most about my first meeting with Alan Curtis is what a unique personality he had. I had the privilege to play under him, and it was a great honour for me to have had him as part of my coaching team. There is a huge need for successful clubs to have a personality like Alan around. Real Madrid had Alfredo di Stéfano, Barcelona had Johan Cruyff, whilst Inter Milan had Luis Suárez. All these clubs had people like Alan Curtis, someone whom the fans could relate to, someone whom they felt could represent them. For me, Alan is that kind of person, a gentle-mannered man who shares with the fans his love for the club.

Not only is Alan a gentleman, but he was a fantastic and skilful player. Unfortunately, I never saw him play live, but I have seen footage, and he would have graced any Swans team in any era. Alan was a player of immense flair, and that is the philosophy of the Swans today.

Alan is a great ambassador for the club and a great example to every young player, showing them what is needed when they represent Swansea City, because he distinguished himself with all four of his league teams and his country. I remember the time Alan demonstrated his profound love for the Swans in the 2002–03 season when we almost dropped out of the Football League. We were away to Rochdale in the penultimate game of the season, and I could see by Alan's face and mood how much it meant to him that the Swans kept our league status. In that game and the last game against Hull, his motivational words made the players aware of what the club means to the people of Swansea and their families.

Alan, I believe, should be with the club for the rest of his life. He has a genuine love for the Swans, and because of the man he is he could fill many roles. He can represent the players, staff and fans in equal measure, such is his love for Swansea City Football Club. In the future, I just hope the Swans can make Alan proud. What they go on to achieve will be a testimony both to him and to the fans. Enjoy the book – Alan has a great story to tell.

Roberto Martínez,
September 2009

1

CWM RHONDDA

30 August 1981 was a momentous day in Swansea for several reasons. First, it was very hot, a notable event in itself for a summer day in the West Wales seaside resort. Second, Swansea City were playing their first-ever home game as a First Division football club. But most remarkably of all, they were leading Leeds United, one of the greats of British football, by four goals to one in front of over 23,000 fans at the Vetch Field.

As the clock began to run down, I picked up the ball on the right-hand touchline halfway inside the Leeds half in front of an already delirious North Bank, and as I looked up I saw that I was being marshalled inside by Trevor Cherry, an England full-back and teammate at Leeds the previous season. As I moved towards the opposition area, Cherry tried to use his experience to push me inside, where the defensive cover awaited to crowd me out. However, on the edge of the Leeds box, I shimmied as if to go inside my marker, cut back outside him and, as three defenders converged on me, let fly. The ball hit the left-hand corner of John Lukic's net.

The vast majority of footballers will tell you how special it is to score against your old team, especially when your spell at that club was perceived by some pundits as being less than successful. The combination of factors that came together on that memorable August day would not be out of place in a *Boy's Own* story. Not only had we won our first-ever First Division home game 5–1, but our opponents had been my previous club Leeds, and I had scored the last goal.

The 1981–82 season proved to be an amazing one for the Swans, as we finished sixth in the league. Even today, I am constantly reminded by Swansea fans of their memories of that season and that goal especially. Although it is perhaps the most documented goal of my playing career, it is just one of hundreds of happy memories I have of my 40-year love affair with the game of football and the city of Swansea in particular.

Despite my close association with Swansea, 'home' will always be the place whose name is synonymous with the industrial history and culture of Wales: the Rhondda Valley. Dylan Thomas famously described Swansea as a 'lovely, ugly town'. I wonder what he would have made of Pentre, the village where I was born and bred. The Welsh word *pentref* usually means village or homestead, but in the case of Pentre it refers to an old farmstead that was situated in the area. This farm was quite substantial in size and was known as Y Pentref long before an actual village grew up in the area with the advent of the mining industry. It was a typical small valleys community, and the geographical features of the area were dominated by the scars of decades of coal mining and its associated industries. It was in one of the rows and rows of two-up, two-down terraced houses, familiar to any South Wales valleys town, that I, Alan Thomas Curtis, entered the world on Good Friday, 16 April 1954, at 17 Madeline Street. I was the second son of Tydfil and Albert, my brother Phillip having been born three years earlier.

In the decades after the Second World War, there was little choice for women like my mother regarding birthing options. There was no agonising decision to make as to whether the prospective mother should opt for a water pool or a Caesarean, or which hospital to choose. It was usually the case that wherever the mother was when labour started, the baby was delivered nearby, nearly always at home. This was no exception for my mother. After she felt her contractions begin, she called for the neighbours, and I was delivered in our front room. My father, however, was unaware of all this commotion at number 17, as he was playing football down the local park. Not for the last time, then, that football would play a part in the Curtis household. He was informed of my imminent arrival by some local boys and got home just as I was being born.

My father loved his football and was an excellent local league player who turned down the chance to play professionally with Leicester City because he was a family man. My mother and his sons meant the world to him, so he didn't want to risk disrupting his young family. Signing professional forms would have meant moving 'abroad' to England, an alien land many miles away from the loving support of his family and friends. Besides, it would not have been a very good career move financially, as footballers at that time were more or less chattels of the club or the chairman, invariably a powerful local businessman, and bound to the chains of the maximum wage. My father, like many men of the Rhondda Valley, decided to take his chances at home mining the 'black gold', the quality coal that was exported worldwide.

At the time my mother and father decided to start a family, the nature of employment in the Valleys was only just beginning to undergo some sort of transformation. The government had attempted to develop a regional policy, part of which was to encourage new factories into the Rhondda to replace those jobs lost by the increasing closure of the pits. I will always remember, however, my father saying that mining was in his family's blood, as was the case on my mother's side of the family.

Like the majority of other families in Pentre and its surrounding area, we could hardly have been described as well off. However, we didn't know any different, so we never moaned, and there didn't seem to be the pressure of the materialism that exists in today's society. Everything families did back then was community based. Women would buy all that was needed at the local shop, passing the time of day with the other mothers and grandmothers. Routines were so predictable that the majority of families never needed a watch – the women's daily and weekly routines were the same: cooking, cleaning, washing and ironing. Perhaps this might seem a tedious lifestyle when looked at today, but at that time it was an expected and integral part of the life of any working-class housewife.

Mam, who married my father when she was 18, however, was not a stereotypical Welsh mother. She could only be described as what I would call a character. She had a fantastic sense of humour and would certainly speak her mind. My father respected her wishes, and it came as no surprise that she carried on working when we grew up. The extra money often found its way towards us in the form of new clothes or the occasional treat. She worked in Polikoffs clothing factory, which later became Burberry's, a major employer until recently when they controversially closed the factory and moved production abroad.

My father and his mates worked long hours in dangerous conditions to provide for their families. Any leisure pursuits they undertook were therefore enjoyed to the maximum. Despite the secularisation of the Valleys in the years after the Second World War, it was still predominantly through churches that organised team games took place. Pentre boasts what is known locally as the 'Cathedral of the Rhondda', St Peters Church, which was consecrated in 1890 and whose impressive tower dominates the local landscape. The 'chapel' was at the top of the social hierarchy – literally, as it was at the top of the street, whilst the Legion club was at the bottom!

It wasn't just the men whose social lives were influenced by the church. For the rest of the family, and particularly the children, the chapels were a vital source of leisure activities, especially the organisation of the annual Sunday school trips to the seaside resorts of Barry Island and Porthcawl. My father played sport, but many of his contemporaries opted for other pastimes that were on offer, those that never involved going outside. They instead chose the hobbies that were offered in the pubs, clubs and billiard halls, such as snooker, darts and cards. The added advantage, of course, of these indoor activities was that they allowed many working-class men to indulge their favourite leisure activity of all, that of partaking in a glass or two of beer. In fact, our village was well known locally for its beer, the Pentre Breweries opening in 1875 and supplying beer to the rest of the Rhondda until it closed in the years following the Second World War.

I first experienced this culture when I was about 16 and my father occasionally sneaked me into the Legion to watch Wales rugby internationals. Well, perhaps more to experience the atmosphere, as you couldn't really see the black-and-white telly for the dense smoke coming from the roll-ups and Woodbines! It was great fun as an impressionable youngster to watch the men have a gamble on the horses and play cards for a few bob. But my father was more of an advocate of the great outdoors, and he would take Phillip and me on walks and encourage us to have a kickaround with him and his mates in the park that was situated in the middle of Pentre. When I was small, the park seemed like a huge stadium, with terraced houses on either side acting like great banks of football terracing. Going back there today, it's hard not to smile at my naivety. I later found out that these amphitheatres, as we thought of them, were man-made as a result of some of the first reclamation schemes in the UK.

If my father was vital in creating my early interest in football, it was another family member who reinforced my growing obsession with the game. My uncle was the Wales international Roy Paul, who captained Manchester City in both the 1955 and 1956 FA Cup finals. Such a notable success story made a big impact in such a close-knit community and was celebrated by everyone. My mother's brother, or Uncle Roy as we called him, had started his career with Swansea Town but had moved on to the bigger stage of the First Division in 1950. He captained the Maine Road side in their 3–1 defeat by Newcastle United in his first cup final, but City exacted revenge the following season, triumphing over Birmingham City by exactly the same scoreline.

I was too young to fully share in this success, but Phillip went on a tour of the local schools with Roy and the rest of the family. It seemed as though every child in the valley had their photo taken with the world's most prestigious knockout trophy and the winning Man City skipper. These days, though, the nearest a child will get to an FA Cup-winning captain is seeing them on *Match of the Day*!

Although it was nearly the case that nobody got to see the cup back in 1956 either. After losing the 1955 final, Uncle Roy had promised that the following year he would lead City to victory and bring the cup back to the Rhondda. After the Wembley victory, he was as good as his word. On the way home, he decided to catch up with a few old mates in the local, and they were of course keen to congratulate him and toast the return of one of the Rhondda's favourite sons. Naturally, everyone was eager to have a few words with the winning cup-final captain and buy him a pint. Roy was a character and happily chatted with the increasing number of locals who packed the pub as news of his return filtered through the village. One or two drinks turned into several more.

The next morning, as Roy woke up and began to recall the night before, an increasing feeling of dread washed over him as he realised he couldn't remember what he had done with the cup. As he trudged back up the hill to the pub where he had left his car, he could probably visualise the terrible newspaper headlines, along the lines of 'Welshman loses the English FA Cup'. When he got to his car, he must have had a double take, as there in the back seat, shining in the early morning sun, was the cup. And what's more, Uncle Roy had even left the car window open!

Even though I was only two when my uncle achieved his greatest success, I would listen in awe over the following years to his many football stories. Like many of his contemporaries, he started his working life down the mine after his initial foray into competitive football was met with rejection. Even though he became a full international, Roy would say that his biggest disappointment was not being selected by Bronllwyn Primary after three schoolyard trials. He insisted that this was an even bigger disappointment than losing the 1955 FA Cup final!

He got over his initial rejection to sign professionally for Swansea Town in 1940 and remained there for nearly a decade. In 1950, he moved to Manchester City, although it was not a straightforward transfer. In fact, his controversial move would not have been out of place in the modern game, with all the accusations today of bungs to agents and alleged under-the-counter payments to players.

The Swans had originally agreed a fee with a club in Bogotá, Columbia, which was almost unheard of at the time, as there was minimum player movement to European clubs let alone ones in South America. The football authorities got wind of the transfer just as Roy landed in Columbia and would not permit him to sign his contract. The West Wales club had lost out on their fee, so it is rumoured they offered Roy a 'sweetener' to speed up his move to the Sky Blues for £19,500, top money in those days. Whatever the truth, City certainly got value for money, as my uncle went on to play over 300 games, scoring 23 goals and helping to bring silverware to the club.

Many people have told me that Roy was a leader of men, a defensive midfielder in the mould of Dave Mackay, Billy Bremner or Roy Keane, although perhaps not as physical as those players. Roy was a charismatic, natural leader, although there are also tales of his more mischievous side, guiding players into bars on foreign trips when they should have been relaxing! My favourite stories as a youngster were when Uncle Roy would tell me about the players he felt it was a privilege to play with. When I started playing professionally myself and was lucky enough to meet them, it was those very same players who told me the privilege was theirs – legends of the game such as the former German prisoner-of-war Bert Trautmann, the keeper who so famously helped City win the cup by playing through the pain barrier with a broken neck, and Don Revie, who would go on to manage at the very highest level with Leeds United and England.

Even though he had been worshipped by the City followers, after leaving top-flight football Roy decided, like so many of his generation, to use his experience to give something back to the game at a lower level. With this in mind, he decided to step down to non-league football with Worcester City in the old Southern League in 1957, only one year after lifting the Cup at Wembley. He stayed with the Midlands club for three years, including a stint at the end as player-manager. However, he did not give up his romance with the FA Cup, as he scored against both Liverpool and Millwall as Worcester went on a giant-killing run in 1959. After this, Roy played local football with Brecon and Garw in the Welsh League before hanging up his boots when he was well into his 40s. As in the case of his Wales international colleague John Charles, Roy was willing to continue in the lower leagues for as long as his body would physically allow him. Both players had graced the world stage yet were prepared to slog it out on local parks with players half their age just because of their sheer love and respect for the game.

It is no wonder that the sport of football was beginning to make such an impression on me. Not many families could boast (not that we would have, of course) an FA Cup-winning captain as one of their own, but to find one in South Wales, a traditionally rugby-oriented region, was indeed a rarity. Talk of my uncle's cup exploits made the competition all the more appealing, and I could not wait for it to begin each year. I would wait anxiously for the draw to see who the South Wales clubs – Cardiff, Swansea, Newport and sometimes, if they got through the qualifying rounds, my nearest 'big' club, Merthyr Tydfil – would be paired with. And, unbelievably, my village club Ton Pentre from the Welsh League would sometimes make it to the first round when Welsh non-league clubs were able to compete in the qualifying rounds of the tournament.

My father's relatively well-paid job meant that the Curtis household had access to a television set, and my interest in football was consolidated by watching the spectacle of the FA Cup final every May. The first final I vividly remember was in 1960 between Wolverhampton Wanderers and Blackburn Rovers, two of the top teams at that time. When the 'Old Gold' (not that we could tell that with our old black-and-white set) of Wolves triumphed, I was an instant fan, perhaps because at that time they were also one of the real glamour clubs. European fixtures were few and far between, with only the league champions entering European competition. In the mid 1950s, Wolves, under their forward-thinking manager Stan Cullis, had arranged friendly fixtures against some of Europe's finest and were able to boast of victories over teams such as Spartak Moscow, Honvéd and Dynamo Moscow.

I was hooked, and it was great to support such a successful team. The only problem for me was that Wolves were knocked out of the following year's competition in the third round by Huddersfield Town. So, what was a young, impressionable and football-loving kid supposed to do? Well, perhaps do what other young boys have done before and since: find another successful team, and who better to support than the glorious Tottenham Hotspur side that won back-to-back FA Cup finals in 1961 and 1962?

Spurs were a great team, and, even better for me, they had three famous Welsh internationals, two of whom were Swansea-born wingers: Cliffy Jones, flying down the left wing, using his pace and bravery to great effect, and Terry Medwin on the right wing – Terry was later to play an important part in my own professional development. They were very different players, but each was highly effective in his own way. For a wide player, Cliff would get his fair share of goals, whilst Terry was more of a play-maker or, as Jimmy Greaves once described him, 'like a piano player in the orchestra'.

Another reason for my early affinity with the White Hart Lane club, and the third Welsh player on their books, was a local Rhondda lad called Mel Hopkins, who was born in Ystrad, less than two miles from Pentre. Mel was a classy left-back who played 34 times for Wales and starred in the 1958 World Cup finals, where in the quarter-final against Brazil he prevented the world-class winger Garrincha from imposing his usual influence on the game.

This great Spurs team must have made a huge impression on me at that early age, as I still look out for their results – just after those of all the Welsh clubs, of course!

A few years later, my love affair with the cup was consolidated when the Swans went on their famous run in 1964 and reached the semi-final. I remember reading the reports of how they beat higher-division opposition Stoke City and Sheffield United in replays at the Vetch Field. In the run up to the quarter-final, there was some divided opinion in the schoolyard. The majority of the Rhondda were followers of Cardiff City and didn't give the Swans much of a chance, as they were away to high-flying Liverpool. Even back then, I liked good football and didn't have an allegiance to any particular Welsh club. I just remember the Swans playing attractive football. I think, like most people, I was stunned when the Swans triumphed at Anfield, but it all ended in tears as Preston won the semi, ultimately losing to West Ham in the final. Swansea keeper Noel Dwyer was hailed as a hero for his performance at Anfield, only to concede a fluke goal from the halfway line against Preston. I made a promise to myself then that I would never, ever play in goal!

By the time I first attended Pentre Junior School, a few hundred yards from our house, I was well and truly mesmerised by the game. However, I sometimes wish I could be seven today, in the age of Premier League football, a sort of reverse of the BBC series *Life on Mars* – instead of being transported back in time, I wish I could have moved forward 30-odd years. Not that my childhood was anything other than wonderful. It is just that I wish I could have had the pick of the plethora of football shirts on offer to the children of today. In my day, you had the choice of a red or a royal-blue shirt, but that didn't stop me from imagining that I was wearing the colours of Manchester United or Everton – or any other famous club that wore those colours. Unfortunately, there were no white tops available in the colour of my beloved Spurs.

A group of youngsters, including me and Phillip, would hone our skills kicking a ball at every opportunity we could: in school breaks, every evening and, apart from an hour or so on a Sunday when we were at chapel, all weekend. I still remember the names of our soccer gang, which included Phillip and Andrew Owen, David Morgan, Peter Williams, Stevie Williams, Alan Harvey and Paul Pumford, all of whom were good players who went on to play successfully for many years in the local leagues. We would all run down to the park straight from school, playing until stopped by darkness or the call from one or more of our mothers to come home for bed. We would start off with three- or four-a-side, but within an hour there could be anything up to eighteen-a-side.

We didn't just play in the park, either, as on winter nights we would have massive games in the street. These were seldom interrupted, as very few people owned a car in Pentre in those days. I always laugh at the Carling Black Label advert on the telly, with those blokes with huge beer bellies playing on the street. It reminds me of our street games as a kid, as all the players were within about two yards of the ball. In all those games, it was my brother Phillip who really stood out – not because he was older, but because he had a sweet left foot. 'Beckenbauer' we used to call him!

Phillip and I were, I suppose, typical brothers. We loved each other to bits and would defend each other to the hilt, but there were three years between us, which meant we also had our own sets of friends. I would say that Phillip helped to toughen me up and gave me a competitive edge – most kids want to put one over on their older sibling.

Close, did I say? Well, we had to be, as we shared the same bed until Phillip left to join the RAF when he was 21. And you have to remember that we did not have central heating in those days. And those Rhondda winters were cold, to say the least!

Although I was becoming increasingly obsessed by football, I was not allowed to neglect my education, as my parents, like most of the Valleys' traditionally working-class families, knew and valued its importance. This could be said of all mining communities, who placed a great emphasis on the social opportunities provided by education. Miners' libraries could be found in all mining areas, with hundreds of books bought by the workers' own contributions and donated to the villages so that everybody, especially the children, could benefit.

My parents encouraged Phillip and me to lead healthy, outdoor lifestyles, but that did not stop us progressing in our studies. Phillip followed my father into Pentre Secondary School, whilst a few years later I passed the eleven-plus and went to the local grammar school, Porth County. My father was a great role model, not only football-wise, but with education. He started his working life as a baker before going to college to gain an apprenticeship to be a fitter underground at Parc and Dare Collieries. When he had a family, he decided to better himself and went to night school at Llwynypia College, where he gained the qualifications to become a lecturer in mechanical engineering.

Communities in Pentre and the wider Rhondda Valley were close-knit, and all the kids had the same hobbies, playing cricket in the summer, with a short break for tennis during Wimbledon fortnight, and football all year round. One particularly notable event occurred every April around Grand National time when we had the Porth's equivalent to Aintree's big race! We would borrow dustbins, make Becher's Brook out of twigs and pinch barrels of beer from Pentre Legion (empty, of course!) to make the rest of the fences. Dozens of kids would then pick the name of a horse and see who would win the

'National'. All the parents would gather and shout encouragement. The old adage 'it is the taking part, not the winning that counts' was borne out at these times.

It was definitely all for one and one for all in the way we spent our spare time, at least until we were 11 years of age. Then came the moment that every kid dreaded: the eleven-plus examination. This could often prove to be very divisive, as boys and girls whom you had grown up with suddenly became categorised as those who were academic and those who were not. Grammar schools have perhaps rightly been attacked for fuelling class divisions and reinforcing the middle classes' position in society. In the Rhondda, though, they could also be argued to have given many youngsters like myself the chance to achieve academic qualifications, offering us the opportunity to secure different types of jobs than those of our fathers and theirs before them.

The problem for me personally was that grammar schools were rugby playing. If you showed any sporting ability, you were made to play rugby for the school in the week and again on Saturday mornings. I was a budding outside-half, like Cliff Morgan and Barry John, and was picked in that position to represent Rhondda Schools. I was also invited to participate in the Welsh Schools trials. As much as I enjoyed my rugby, the round-ball game was always my real passion – perhaps not unexpected when I had an uncle who had been a successful professional footballer and a dad who could have become one as well.

By then, I had joined Treorchy Boys Club, and playing rugby on Saturday morning and football in the afternoon was taking its toll. One had to go, so at 14 rugby was kicked into touch! There were some good players at grammar school: Dai Edwards, Terry Broome, Neil Roberts and Keith 'Tassie' Evans. Again, like my mates in junior school, they never progressed to the professional game, but they did enter white-collar professions: Dai Davies became an optician and Dickie Tudball still has an estate agents in Treorchy.

One of the other great things I remember about growing up was the more than healthy competition that existed between the Rhondda Valleys villages, whether it was in the field of sport or singing. Nearly every village had an excellent choir, such as the Treorchy Male Voice, who were renowned and won many competitions, travelling the length of the country. In fact, my father and his brother Hedley were both members of the Treorchy choir.

The other great memory I have of childhood is the annual pilgrimage to the seaside that the majority of Valleys families made in the last week of July and the first week of August every summer. Can you imagine? We would live side by side, sometimes in each other's houses, for fifty weeks of the year, then for two weeks in the summer would head for Trecco Bay in Porthcawl for the miners' 'stop fortnight', only to spend time next to each other in rows of caravans rather than terraced houses. My mother was one of fourteen children, which meant I had a vast array of cousins who along with our friends all participated in the mass exodus to the coast. Every year, Pentre became like a ghost town for that fortnight, but not much changed for the children. Instead of playing on grass, we played on sand. For the boys, it was like playing on Copacabana Beach in Rio de Janeiro, usually minus both the glorious sunshine and the subtle skill levels of Brazilian football.

The start of my rewarding journey in the game began at the age of 11 in Treorchy, a village very similar to the one I was brought up in, only a mile away. Here, as in Pentre, everyone looked out for each other. It was this spirit that made us such a good side. Like most successful teams at any level of the game, we were encouraged to develop an 'us and them' mentality. I spent six happy years at the club and am eternally grateful for the excellent coaching and grounding in the game that I was given.

Like any other junior club up and down the country, parental involvement was vital. My father was no exception to this rule, especially given his earlier successes playing the game. An added bonus was that my dad owned one of the few cars in the village at the time, a Morris Minor. Every Saturday, he would cram us all into his car and chauffeur us back and forth to the game. It's a good job that there was only one substitute allowed per team at that time! Dad had never thought about getting a car before I started playing football, as work at the mine was only a hundred or so yards from our terraced house. The fact that in his mid-30s he bought one demonstrated to me even at a young age how committed he was to my succeeding in the game, and this only made me more determined never to let him down.

The club I played for was in essence a youth club, a place where boys and girls would meet up for a chat or a game of table tennis. Football, although important, was just another part of the facility. The person who oversaw the club and dedicated his life to it was Albie Nicholas. He did everything from organising fixtures, marking the pitches and washing the kit to making the half-time tea. Politicians today are constantly calling for ordinary people who dedicate their lives to others to be rewarded with either an OBE or MBE. Albie was certainly someone who fell into this category, and he deservedly received a British Empire Medal, presented to him by the late Bill Owen of *Last of the Summer Wine* fame. Sadly, Albie is no longer with us, but he lived well into his 90s. When he passed away, generations of people from the Valleys turned up in their hundreds to pay their respects to his positive contributions to their lives.

I look back with fondness at my time with Treorchy, but perhaps also a little through rose-tinted glasses. I remember us being a great team, but we never actually won a trophy! My excuse is that we only included boys from the surrounding villages in our team, whilst teams such as Ystrad Rhondda would head hunt the cream of talented youngsters, the Rhondda Valley's equivalent of a modern-day Chelsea! They would bring in boys from further afield, luring the better players from other teams. Towards the end of my time at school, the rules stopping grammar-school pupils from playing football were relaxed, which meant I was able to represent Rhondda Schools in competitive matches throughout South Wales. I even had the privilege of captaining the team on several occasions.

My coaches made me aware that my performances were attracting the attention of some Football League clubs, such as Bristol Rovers and Leicester City, who had unsuccessfully courted my father years before, although Swansea City were the most persistent. They sent Geoff Ford, one of their main scouts, to watch us play against West Glamorgan, and afterwards Swansea offered me a trial.

Although Swansea's interest was very exciting, it also created a bit of a dilemma for me, as I was doing fairly well academically. I was really unsure as to whether I should focus on becoming a professional footballer, with all the uncertainties that were involved, or concentrate fully on my studies, which would hopefully provide me with the education to get a white-collar job rather than tread the well-worn path to the local colliery. The advice of my family, particularly my father, proved invaluable. Whilst a good education didn't necessarily guarantee a good job, he told me, it was a lot less risky than a career in football, which was an extremely precarious profession. Yes, there were success stories such as Uncle Roy, but for every Roy Paul, Cliff Jones or Terry Medwin there were thousands of other boys who had been discarded at 17 or 18 with no qualifications and had no choice but to return home to a life underground or working on factory conveyor belts. My father was not being derogatory; he knew of the dangers and drudgery of these jobs, as he had made that difficult choice himself. In the end, we reached a compromise, because in all honesty my mind was still set on becoming a footballer.

A trainee footballer's wage in the early 1970s was much the same as what I could have expected for working underground, so a contract did not mean a life of luxury. There were no six-figure sums on offer as incentives to parents to get their sons to sign on the dotted lines – not that my parents would have been so easily won over by such incentives anyway. So, it was decided that I would continue at the grammar school for another two years and study for my A levels, with the added bonus that as a sixth-former I would be able to opt to play either rugby or football.

It was in sixth form that I came under the tutelage of my history teacher Mr Thomas, or 'Dai Chips' after the teacher in the film *Goodbye, Mr Chips*. Dai was a massive football fan, so he gave up hours of his time, as teachers did then, in order to run the school team on evenings and weekends.

Life couldn't have been better. I was doing well at school, and I was also playing football at a good level, having already had a few games in the Welsh League with Ferndale. As a slender 16 year old, this was a great grounding for what was to come as a professional. The league was littered with ex-pros who did not take kindly to some upstart trying to go round them. There was many a time I would end up on my backside, up in the air or up against the perimeter fence. Not once did I retaliate – not that I did not want to, but some of them seemed as big as the mountains I'd climbed a few years before! It was, in part, this experience that led to me winning an Under-18 international cap for Wales.

After a close season of playing cricket and the annual two weeks to Porthcawl, I returned to school for the second year of my A levels. The Swans seemed as determined as ever to sign me, often coming to watch me play for the school or in the Welsh League, but I was happy to go along with the family's wish of getting my qualifications first. For the next year, I worked hard at my school work and football, and I eventually gained A-level passes in history and economics and was accepted into teacher training college.

The Swans were putting pressure on me to attend trials, and the buzz I got on the pitch far outweighed what I felt with my head in a text book, so a crisis meeting was called in the Curtis household. A decision had to be made: college or football? There was no guarantee that I would make it as a professional footballer, but becoming a fully qualified teacher was not a certainty either. So, with the blessing of my parents, I decided that it was football for me, although I did feel a tinge of guilt at my decision.

The same year, Phillip left home to join the RAF, so within months my mother and father had 'lost' two sons. The Curtis household rapidly changed from one with two bustling teenagers to one of relative quiet. All that was left was to pack my bags and accept the offer of a trial with Swansea City, then in the depths of the old Third Division. Surely things could only get better for the club, and I was determined that I was going to do my utmost to realise my own ambition of playing in the First Division and to help raise the Swans from the doldrums. In reality, it could never be done . . . could it?

2

AN UGLY, LOVELY TOWN

I left Pentre in the summer of 1972, hoping that I was embarking on a long and successful career in the game. As with most trainee footballers, I aimed to fulfil my boyhood dreams of playing top-flight domestic and international football. And who better to achieve those ambitions with than Swansea City, one of my local teams?

Over the years, the Swans had developed a reputation for playing a good brand of pass-and-move football and for producing talented individuals, many of whom excelled at international level. However, when I joined them, they were struggling at the wrong end of the Third Division.

Swansea might have only been down the road, but it felt like the other side of the world to me! Today, the journey takes about an hour, but in 1972 it was very different, as the M4 network had yet to be completed. This meant it took more than an hour to get to Port Talbot and sometimes just as long again to get through the old town, with its famous steelworks, and on to Swansea. By rail took just as long, as you had to change trains three times!

It was a Saturday morning when I packed my bags for the journey west, and I still remember it vividly, as the Curtis house was full of well-wishers, friends and family, all ready to offer me their own snippets of advice. There were only about 20 houses in our street, but it seemed as though the whole village had turned up to bid me farewell. Our next-door neighbours, Mrs Hendy, Mrs Williams, Mrs Harvey, and Cyril and Joan Davies, were all there. Even today when I return to Pentre I think of that day, as there are reminders everywhere of how much some things haven't changed. Mrs Hendy's daughters Karen and Janice still live next to their parents' home, Mrs Harvey's daughters Lisa and Alison have moved into their mother's, Peter Williams lives in his family's home, and Cyril and Joan still live in the same house.

That morning, my mates told me how excited they were at the prospect of coming down to the big city for a night out, although my mother soon put me right on that score – I was a village boy and was to look out for all those girls who chase footballers, especially in a big city such as Swansea! Mam could have given a few tips to today's Premier League stars before they go out on their Christmas parties, which can sometimes end in bad publicity for both the club and the players. Dad then offered me advice on sobriety. I was going to be a professional athlete, which did not mix, he insisted, with drinking copious amounts of alcohol – sound advice that I have followed to this day. As for Mam's advice? Well, I'd rather not say!

Uncle Roy was also there to see me off, and he too offered me some words of wisdom. Having moved back to the Rhondda, he had quietly kept an eye on my progress but had never interfered, perhaps thinking to have done so would have added pressure or burdened my development, as not many kids have an uncle who had captained an FA Cup-winning team. To be fair, when I was starting out professionally, being the 'nephew of Roy Paul' did have its advantages and perhaps gave me a little bit of a head start when scouts were watching matches.

What he said to me that day amongst all the commotion has stuck with me throughout my time in the game: 'Listen to all the advice that you can get, but try to weed out the bad and take in the good!' It was up to me to discern between the two, but I should listen to and trust the more senior players. It was important to keep an eye out in training to see who took things seriously and who were the good trainers and follow their advice in particular.

My uncle's words have held me in good stead over the years, and I'm still very grateful to him. I have also tried to pass on these words of wisdom to all those youngsters who have come under my tutelage as a coach, and I hope they've proved as beneficial to them as they were for me.

When I arrived at the club, I was not going into a totally alien environment, as I had played quite a few times for the Swans youth team when I was in sixth form. The structure of football was entirely different in those days, with the club having teams in every division of the local pyramid. A player would start off in youth football in the Swansea League and, depending on their development, could rise up the ranks to the first team. Then there were the Swansea Senior League, Welsh League and Football Combination sides to negotiate before you could make the step up to the senior squad. I think this measured progress helped us to develop physically, because there were some hard players with years of experience in these leagues and quite a few had played professionally. Many good players had not made the grade themselves, so maybe had a bit of a grudge or a point to prove and were therefore unwilling to give those of us aspiring to move on an easy time of it. Even if you eventually made it to the first team, there was nothing to stop you ending up back in the Senior League. In fact, it was quite common to see an old pro helping the youngsters at this level.

As a schoolboy, I never played in the Swansea Senior League, as I started off with the Welsh League side. Another player who signed for the Swans at the same time as me did play for both the Senior League and Welsh League teams. He was a rugged centre-half who later quit the Swans to play rugby – his name was Geoff Wheel.

Many a striker was saved from a torrid afternoon by that decision, as Geoff's rugby career saw him win 32 caps for Wales during the glory years of the 1970s.

Playing at the lower levels was certainly a good grounding for any aspiring youngster, as the local leagues helped you develop physicality, and a higher level of technical skill and ball control was required in the Combination. All the southern First Division sides, including Spurs, West Ham, Chelsea and Arsenal, were represented, so as a teenager I faced players of the calibre of Spurs' Cyril Knowles, Alan Mullery, Phil Beale, Martin Chivers and Joe Kinnear, and I remember playing against Arsenal's Charlie George.

Many of those players had or went on to represent their countries, so as a youngster it was a great learning experience. Our manager at Swansea, Roy Bentley, had been captain of the last Chelsea side to win the old First Division title in 1954–55, before Roman Abramovich's wealth made such an impact at the club. Roy knew how important it was to play the youngsters in a league where most of the reserve teams we competed against, I would argue, could have beaten the majority of first teams in the old Third and Fourth Divisions. Roy also used to play the more experienced players along with those youngsters who were knocking on the first-team door, such as Wyndham Evans, Lyn Davies, Phil Holme and Alan Williams, as well as Rhondda lads Keith Evans, Steve Ivins and Terry Broome.

Combination matches helped develop my game as well as giving me a first insight into the real world of professional football, as we were treated relatively well, especially in the away games in London. We would have lunch on the train and dinner on the way back, although 'dinner' usually meant the senior lads getting legless by the time we reached Cardiff. As for us youngsters, we were reminded of our place in the hierarchy, as we had to lug the kit on the Underground between Paddington and whichever ground we were playing at.

Roy's selection policy, especially outside of the first team, wasn't too dissimilar to today's managers, particularly Rafael Benítez, who is renowned for his squad rotation at Liverpool. Many other top-flight managers also pick 'horses for courses', especially in cup competitions. The manager was so desperate for the club to be successful at any level that he was even prepared to select us more experienced players in a West Wales Youth Cup game if it meant bringing some silverware to the Vetch. Even though it helped towards my medal collection, I have to admit I felt sorry for the local boys who represented the Swans on a non-contract basis in the bread-and-butter league games. I remember a guy by the name of Robert Palmer from Townhill who played successfully in the majority of games only to be dropped for an important league or cup game. I suppose this is the reality of life as a professional, be it as a manager or player – tough decisions have to be made, and some players are going to be upset.

This is also the dilemma that faced Brian Flynn as manager of Wales Under-21 in 2008 when his team came close to qualifying for the UEFA European Under-21 Championship. Many of his squad had already successfully progressed to the full international side. Flynn had to decide whether to stick with the team that had got Wales that far or call in the players with greater experience who were still eligible for the Under-21s. As it happened, John Toshack, the Wales manager, and Flynny agreed on the important impact qualification would have for Welsh football and that some of the players who had gained full caps should 'step down', although some people might argue that this was not fair on the players who had got us this far. Football can be a game of tough decisions.

Although Swansea reminded me a lot of my home in the Rhondda Valley, especially the city's landscape, which was also scarred by industrialisation, there were also differences. Rhondda was a close-knit community, whereas Swansea seemed to me to be more cosmopolitan, with a mixture of an indigenous population and those who had come to south-west Wales in search of work in the zinc-smelting, iron and copper works and the docks. Swansea was a small village in the nineteenth century but was turned into a thriving and bustling community during the first two decades of the twentieth century. Unfortunately, the inhabitants of the town had to pay a large price for this rapid industrialisation, as it became infamous as one of the most derelict and polluted areas in Britain, ravaged by industries that continually spewed their pollution into the air, land and water. These environmental factors could have been indirectly responsible for the size of the local football league, which was the second largest in Britain behind Birmingham, as the local football park was probably the safest place for kids to play.

After leaving home, my first digs were with Harry Griffiths, one of the coaches at the Vetch, and his wife Gwen. Whilst my parents were irreplaceable, Harry and Gwen were the next best thing. I sometimes had pangs of homesickness, but they helped me through the difficult times. It also helped that another lodger, Dai Davies, was from the Rhondda. Dai was a centre-forward, and although he was released by the Swans after a few years, he did go on to play professionally with Crewe.

The Swans used many landladies throughout the city, but I was really fortunate to be with Gwen, who was like a second mother to me. After I left the Griffiths' household, she took in many more youngsters, whom I know she treated exactly the same. It was almost as much of a wrench to leave Gwen's when I married as it was to leave Madeline Street.

When I lived at home, my father and I would often talk about how my football career was developing, but we also discussed my academic progress and life in general. With Harry, though, it was football 24/7, as he lived and breathed the game. He was both my landlord and coach, so there was no escape from football even if I wanted it. We would have breakfast together, he would give me a lift to training in his Ford Cortina, he would train and coach me, and then I would have to hang around for a lift home after he had finished his other duties. Although I don't suppose I really had to wait, because we only lived half a mile or so from the ground – it was really my choice to do so. I used to stay and use the time to good effect, going behind the North Bank, hitting ball after ball against the wall. Left foot, right foot, long and short passes: I was going to be the complete player. Practice was definitely going to make perfect, although I don't know what happened with my left foot!

Harry had told me about Ivor Allchurch, arguably the Swans' greatest player of all time, and how he would practise endlessly after training, trying to perfect his technique. If it was good enough for the golden boy of Swansea football history, it was certainly good enough for Alan Curtis! I have since encouraged all the kids who I have coached to practise as much as they can, even on their own. Gary Player, one of the finest golfers of all time, famously said, 'The more I practise, the luckier I seem to get!'

Up until the inception of the Premier League, you could argue that every team had a favourite son, a 'Mr Leeds United', 'Mr Tottenham Hotspur' or 'Mr Liverpool', a player or coach who gave his all to a club and spent a lifetime in service to it. With the exception of Ryan Giggs and a few others, loyalty to one club is increasingly harder to find in the modern game. At all levels of the game, players now switch teams more frequently, whether it be for better contracts, to be closer to their families or whatever. When I started out, 'Mr Swansea City' was Harry Griffiths. He might have been small in stature, but he had a huge heart and an immense love for his home-town club. After joining the club at 15, he fulfilled every role, as a player, coach, chief scout, assistant manager, manager and even physio. As a player, he represented the Swans in every position, bar goalkeeper and centre-half, and scored 68 goals in 424 league appearances. What a servant and what a man!

Nice guys, it is often quoted, finish last, but Harry was a nice guy and also had a successful career in the game. Despite his softer side, he was prepared to tell any player what was what if he felt they were trying to cut corners or take unfair advantage of him. Harry and my uncle Roy had played together for club and country, but if I thought

I could get away with things because of Harry's respect for and friendship with my uncle, I was wrong. Harry would often reminisce at home about his playing days with Roy, but in training and during games I quickly found out that there were to be no favourites.

As well as offering words of encouragement, Harry could also be your biggest critic. I remember after one game I trudged off the field to be greeted by Harry, who thought I had not played particularly well. 'The nephew of Roy Paul? More like his niece,' he bellowed as I made my way down the tunnel. In fairness, though, he would offer praise and encouragement just as easily.

Also on the coaching staff was Roy Saunders. Signed from Liverpool as a midfielder, Roy loved his football, and his enthusiasm for the game held no bounds. If we were having a kickaround after training, Roy would join in with his suit on. It was hilarious watching him fall arse over tit trying to make tackles in his platform shoes. When we were knocking balls in to the keeper, Roy would be challenging for them with his overcoat on!

As well as his enthusiasm, Roy had a great knowledge of the game, and this rubbed off on his son Dean. As a kid, Dean showed great potential and was signed by the Swans, only to be released by John Bond. Deano then had a trial for Cardiff but was not taken on by the Ninian Park club. After being out of the game for over a year with a serious ligament injury, he finally got his chance at Brighton, where he became a regular goal scorer, going on to represent his country and play at the highest level with, amongst others, Aston Villa and Liverpool. Dean is the perfect example to youngsters today who are not offered a contract or are released by a club, as he worked hard, always keeping fit and making sure that when an opportunity came along he was in the frame. Dean was highly regarded by his fellow professionals because of what he went on to achieve in the game, which will obviously help him to gain the respect of his own players at Wrexham, his first managerial position. As well as being a top player and coach, he is also a very funny guy and a fantastic impersonator. When he takes off Tosh, he is more like Tosh than the real thing!

My first six weeks of pre-season training alerted me to the importance the club placed on fitness. I believed myself to be reasonably fit. After all, I was a teenager who had spent most of my waking hours running around kicking a football down the park with my mates or training two nights a week with my local club. However, being a full-time professional was something else. I was amazed how my fitness levels rose in those first few weeks of training every day.

Players today often moan about the training facilities if the grass has not been cut the right way or if the showers are not hot or cold enough. When I started out, we didn't even have a training pitch. We had to borrow the university's pitches on Fairwood Common, which the club continued to do until the recent move to what is a relatively state-of-the-art facility at Llandarcy.

There was a particular emphasis on running as a means of getting fit, which was not always to the liking of some of the more senior pros. I remember my old teammate Leighton Phillips telling me about his first pre-season at Cardiff City. The City manager Jimmy Scoular ordered the squad to run from Ninian Park up Leckwith Hill and back again, a run of around eight to ten miles. As they were getting back to the ground, a scrap-metal lorry passed them. The lorry stopped and out jumped Mel Charles, who had got one of his firm's lorry drivers to take him around the circuit. Charlo arrived before Scoular but, unfortunately for him, fell out, broke his ankle and was out for six weeks. I bet the dour Scot Jimmy was not a happy man!

Such antics also went on at the Swans. Every Monday, we would run from the Vetch Field to Knab Rock in Mumbles to touch the 'Apple' and back again, a run of about 15 miles. To make sure we got to Mumbles, Harry would drive down or Roy Saunders would cycle if it was a nice day. The coaches would ensure we touched the tourist landmark before setting off on the return leg. But they did not know the tricks the senior players such as Tony Millington, Barrie Hole and Geoff 'Janna' Thomas got up to on the 'run' back. They would hitch a ride with a passing lorry, car or even milk float and would be dropped off a mile or so from the Vetch. They would then sprint as fast as they could before being met by the coaching team, sweating profusely and gasping for breath. The younger, more naive players would jog in half an hour or so later to be greeted with howls of laughter from the senior pros. In all fairness to them, they had paid their dues over the years and were maybe winding down after a long career. Back then, they played 40 or 50 games a season, and squad rotation at first-team level had not been heard of, so many played more than 500 games throughout their career. Sports science was also an alien concept, but I guess the training methods did work, as we were always kept in excellent physical shape for what was an arduous season on pitches that had lost all of their grass by the end of September!

The majority of our pre-season work did not involve a football at all, which I thought was a bit strange at first, as that is what we were meant to be doing on a Saturday come August. We would often be into the fourth or fifth week of training before we actually started to kick a ball. When we did, there was no better place to do so than at Three Cliffs Bay on the Gower, one of the most beautiful beaches in Britain. We would be dropped off by bus in Penmaen, run down the hill and then have a game on the beach. I remember going down there one day when it was well into the 80s. As we got off the bus in our training kit, I looked around and saw Geoff putting on his tracksuit bottoms. I could not believe it, as it was sweltering, so I asked him why on earth he was wearing a tracksuit. 'Where else am I going to keep my fags, son?' was his reply.

I was three-quarters of the way into my first pre-season, and as I sat on the beach watching Swansea's finest footballers my mind drifted back to my front room and the advice Uncle Roy had given me about trusting the senior players. I do not think he had this in mind. Still, it was great fun, there was a good camaraderie amongst us and I was beginning to discern what, for me, were good or bad training habits.

Geoff was a terrific midfielder, so much so that he once had a loan spell at Old Trafford. I do not know the reason why he did not sign, because he was a good all-round player who had an amazing long shot and regularly scored stunning goals from more than 25 yards out. I could empathise with him about not making it at Old Trafford, because I had a trial there as a 13 year old. Kelvin Davies, a local youngster, and I had been invited up by Jimmy Murphy, the assistant manager and another Pentre boy. I had gone more or less to keep Kelvin company, as so often as not happened in those days. We were both unsuccessful and returned home to the local Rhondda League.

Maybe it was some of his idiosyncrasies that stopped Geoff from gracing the top division. For example, on occasion he would be found having a pint and playing darts with the locals in The White Rose in Mumbles the night before a match! He used to say it was because he couldn't sleep before a game – it was his way of relaxing. But the club was not that rigid in imposing the rules of not drinking after a Thursday night anyway, because some of the coaching staff would join him there, even forming a card school from time to time.

After a rigorous couple of months of pre-season, I was raring to go, although I wasn't too surprised that with my lack of experience I didn't make the starting XI for the opening first-team fixture of the season. But I did not have to wait long for my first taste of Third Division football, as a few injuries meant I made my debut away to Southend United towards the end of August 1972. Another debutant that day was Micky Lenihan, a Swansea-born lad who combined a part-time contract with the Swans with a job as a postman. You do not see that kind of thing happening too much today, with even many non-league players on full-time contracts.

The game pretty much passed me by, and I do not have a clear recollection of it all. One thing I do remember is that both the *Western Mail* and *South Wales Evening Post* had been predicting my inclusion for a couple of days leading up to the game, so I was prepared when I got the nod from Roy Bentley. I also recall two of the opposing players. One was Peter Taylor, who went on to play and manage at the highest level with England, and the other a man-mountain of a centre-forward called Bill Garner, who was later transferred to Chelsea for the not insignificant sum of £100,000. We lost 3–1, with Garner banging one in, so it was not the most pleasing of debuts, and to make matters worse I was subbed with 20 minutes or so to go.

I have often been asked by young players coming through the system to give them advice on what to expect on making their debuts. The only thing I tell them is to prepare as much as possible. I thought I was prepared both physically and mentally for my first professional match, but the one thing that caught me out that night was the pace of the game and how little time I had to dwell on the ball. Night-time matches generate a better atmosphere and perhaps made it appear that the game was quicker than it actually was. As I put on my tracksuit top and sat in the dugout after being substituted, I resolved that I would adapt to the pace of the game more quickly if I ever had the chance again.

We were up against Charlton Athletic next, and as a few players had recovered from injury, I dropped down to the bench. It was more surprising, though, that despite losing 6–0, the manager never saw fit to bring me on. I was only 18 years of age, just starting out in the game, and the manager was a former England international and skipper of a championship-winning side. I did not, therefore, have the temerity to ask him why I was not going on, even though it was pretty obvious that a fresh pair of legs couldn't have made the situation much worse. After the game, though, Roy offered me an explanation for his decision: he did not want me subjected to such a strong and physical side, believing it was in my best interests to watch and learn. Perhaps more surprising was his second reason, which I found astonishing: he said that he wanted to make the players suffer and teach them a lesson by playing with the same team for the full 90 minutes. I obviously wanted to play in every game and did not agree with his decision but put it down to experience.

Roy Bentley was a typical manager of that era, a man who liked nothing better than to pull on his tracksuit and get fully involved in training. As a leading ex-player, he commanded respect and had a real presence. It was also a time when children were taught respect and to never question authority. I was told by my parents, whilst not to be totally reverential, to have respect for others. So although I was never afraid of the manager, I would not question his decision-making and, as with all the other youngsters on the books, would never think of answering him back.

All of the training and most of the coaching were delegated to Harry and Roy Saunders, with Bentley fine tuning the tactics and team selection. What the manager did get involved in were training games, be it five-a-side or full-scale practice matches. State-of-the-art artificial pitches were unheard of back then, with no carpet-like surfaces to play on. The Vetch pitch had to be kept for match days in order for it to last the season, and as we had no training facilities these training games were played behind the North Bank stand on a concrete surface, much the same as any child up and down the country having a kickabout in the schoolyard. The difference being that it was not a kickaround but a fully committed, physical confrontation between players hoping to get the manager's nod for the following Saturday's game.

Rather than discourage us, Bentley used to take part, putting himself in goal. On one side of the stand, the toilet block would be a goal, whilst at the other end a door frame was used, and the manager would position himself there whilst we hammered shots at him from point-blank range. We used to play in shorts and trainers, and people would slide in to make tackles. Bentley, meanwhile, would demonstrate his considerable strength by fending off our shots with his legs, chest, arms and sometimes his face, and not once did I see him flinch. Perhaps this was one of the reasons we never questioned his judgement.

To make sessions even more competitive, he would select the teams, and on many occasions it was Wales versus England, which only served to increase the intensity. He would kick the ball onto the roof of the stand – once the ball dropped, the game commenced. There was only one rule and that was that there weren't any! Elbows would be flying and over-the-top tackles committed, and the competition was fierce. Incredibly, we used to do this on the morning of a match as well, and it was amazing no one suffered a serious injury. The reason behind the manager's thinking, I believe, was to teach us not to dwell on the ball. I could have told him that I learned that lesson after my debut and did not need a forearm smash to remind me. As an 18 year old I was slowly yet surely being introduced to the rigours of the professional game.

Even though I was a peripheral figure in our quest for Third Division survival during the 1972–73 season, I was noticed by the Wales Youth coaching staff, and in the March of my first season as a pro I was selected by Mike Smith, the manager, for my international debut against Scotland. Mike brought a more professional attitude to the Wales set-up and was later deservedly rewarded by replacing Dave Bowen as manager of the full side. Mike was a good organiser, and we benefited under his regime from better training facilities and being supplied with training kit and better hotels.

On the domestic front, my dreams of playing top-level football might not have been going totally to plan, but at least my international prospects seemed to be more promising. As a kid, I had dreamed of representing my country, and I had visions of running out at one of the top First Division grounds, or at least one of the four Welsh clubs in the Football League. It came as a bit of an anticlimax, therefore, when the letter arrived from the Welsh FA informing me that my dream debut was to be at the Pen-y-pound ground, Abergavenny! No disrespect to Abergavenny Thursdays, but this was typical of the way the governing body approached fixtures, although Mark Hughes did insist on, and was granted, much better facilities when he took over the full side years later, and these improved conditions have certainly filtered down to the Under-21s, Under-19s and Under-17s in recent years.

Despite the initial disappointment of not playing at a bigger venue, I was determined to give my best effort, as I was representing my country. Admission to the match was free – although the programme did cost 2p – but even that did not attract many spectators, and the game was played in front of family and friends mostly. The majority of them seemed to belong to the Curtis clan, which wasn't surprising, as we were a very large family, especially on my mother's side. The team that day was K. Bamsey, J.P. Jones, B.W. Griffiths, M.F. Hancock, B. Thomas (Capt), L. Tibbott, A. Curtis, D.M. Williams, R. Jenkins, I. Edwards and M.R. Thomas.

Joey Jones went on to play with great success both at home and abroad with Liverpool and the full Wales side. However, as I looked across the dressing-room at what appeared to be skin pulled over bones, I did not think he had the physique to make it to the very top. Perhaps Joey still thinks I am not a very good judge of players! Les Tibbott went on to play for Coventry, and Ian Edwards also had a successful career in the game. Mickey Thomas, the number 11 that day, also forged a great career in the game, going on to perform at the highest level with many clubs, including Man United. Sitting in the dressing-room that day, I would never have thought that Mickey would have ended up with so much fame and fortune. And he is the first to admit he would have made so much more if the police had not found the printing machine! Mickey was a great character, both on and off the field, although his off-the-field antics did, allegedly, drive many a manager to despair, and I think the title of his recent autobiography gives a good insight into his career: *Kickups, Hiccups and Lockups*. Another member of the team that day was Dave Williams, who went on to play for Bristol Rovers and Norwich before coaching with Manchester United, Chelsea and the Welsh senior team. Dave now works alongside Brian Flynn and me coaching the Welsh youngsters.

The rest of my first season was something of a steep learning curve, experiencing the demands of professional football, albeit in the third tier of the game. I was in and out of the side and never once had a settled run. I think this was partly to do with my inexperience and partly the poor overall performances of the team. We struggled in the lower reaches of the division, and to be fair to Bentley it seemed as though he didn't want the younger players to be too closely associated with the problems of a relegation fight. I think I played only a dozen or so games so did not contribute as much as I would have wanted, and I was disappointed not to get off the mark on the scoring front.

The game that stands out for me in particular was when we were losing away from home and the other team had a player injured. (I was on the bench yet again!) It was a bitterly cold night, so the opposition decided not to send a sub on. Even though we could not beat them with only ten players, I do not know what made Roy react the way he did. Perhaps he thought the opposition were taking the mickey out of us, or maybe he thought we were a right bunch of useless so-and-sos? Whatever the reason, I had never seen the manager as worked up as he was that day. In fact, that was the first time I had seen a grown man lose his temper. He gave us the 'hairdryer' treatment, à la Sir Alex Ferguson, ripping in to us and throwing cups of tea all over the dressing-room.

If he thought his performance would help us to raise our games for the rest of the season, it didn't. Results continued to be poor, and Roy was sacked before the season's end to be replaced by another Harry, this time Gregg of Manchester United and Northern Ireland fame. With all these Roys and Harrys, it was somewhat confusing. One thing is certain, though: it was not the last time that I would witness change at my beloved Vetch Field!

3

THE TWO HARRYS

A change of manager can often have an immediate impact and a team that has previously struggled can suddenly put together a run of much-improved results, as was the case when Harry Redknapp took over the reins at Spurs in 2008. Unfortunately, without the luxury of time and money to spend, Harry Gregg was unable to turn things around, and we were duly relegated to the Fourth Division along with Rotherham, Brentford and Scunthorpe.

In the depths of despair, there was one shining light for the club, as Gregg gave a debut to a promising 16 year old by the name of Robbie James, who would go on to achieve legendary status with the Vetch Field faithful. Robbie's first game was against Charlton, who had drubbed us 6–0 earlier in the season. I had already seen Robbie play in many trials and schoolboy games, having accompanied Harry Griffiths to matches where he would run the rule over players. Even at the tender age of 17, I guess I could have classed myself as an assistant scout. Wherever Harry went, the young Curtis was always in tow!

After watching Robbie, Harry was convinced that the Swans had unearthed a real gem, and I also felt that he would go far in the game. As we both lined up against Charlton for the last game of the 1972–73 season, I do not suppose either of us imagined what we would go on to achieve, especially as we found ourselves in a struggling side that was about to be relegated. We beat Charlton 2–1, and both Robbie and I played in wide attacking roles – him on the right and me on the left. Amongst the despondency of relegation, there was, therefore, some hope for the future. However, before the upturn, there was to be further humiliation.

Even though I was a peripheral member of the first team, the club was a close-knit one, and we all felt the pain of relegation, from the tea lady to the chairman. The relegation was especially disappointing because the Swans had some great players at the time, such as Geoff Thomas and Alan Williams, an uncompromising, yet skilful centre-half, and some promising youngsters, such as Robbie, who were showing potential in the youth set-up. There was also the one and only Swansea-born Herbie Williams, who was a true fans' favourite and hero at the Vetch. Herbie was a member of the famous Swansea schoolboys' team that beat Manchester in the final of the 1954 English Schools Trophy and played over 500 games for the club, scoring 104 goals. During his career, he had countless offers to sign for top teams and was a regular at Wales Under-23 level. Three full caps nowhere near reflected his true ability. If he had transferred to a top team, I am convinced he would have won many more caps than he actually did. Herbie stayed loyal not only to the Swans, but also to his local community in Port Tennant. He was one of the best professionals I have ever played with, and this includes some of the star names and many hardworking pros at all four of my clubs over the years – I can pay Herbie no greater compliment than that.

I am often reminded about the time Herbie lost one of his contact lenses down the Vetch, and the referee stopped the game until it was found, resulting in a hilarious scene, with all the Swans players, the opposition and both coaching staffs on their hands and knees searching for the misplaced lens. What was probably more amazing was that despite all the mud it was found and the game restarted. I suppose if Herbie had been paid what he was worth, he could have bought a spare set!

Like most players, Herbie had superstitions and idiosyncrasies. When Harry Gregg was the manager, the players were allowed a tot of whisky before running out. Herbie would inevitably be first in the queue, then he would appear in the middle of the line before reappearing at the end for the dregs. After that, he would sit down to take out his teeth and put in his contacts. Such were his brilliant performances week in and week out, the management team overlooked it.

Despite having the nucleus of a good side, the players' futures were shrouded in uncertainty. When a new manager arrives, he often doesn't rate a player the same way as his predecessor did. The club also had to take stock, and the board had to take into account the loss of revenue after relegation, so at the end of the 1972–73 season many players were obviously concerned about their contracts. No one more so than me, as I had come to the end of my one-year contract, which had rewarded me with £20 a week basic pay and £5 in appearance money.

The first two weeks of the close season back in Pentre were fraught to say the least, as I wondered if the new manager deemed me capable of making a contribution to the club's rebuilding plans. I knew that the coaching staff had confidence in my ability, but the person who really mattered, Harry Gregg, knew little of me, as I had played only 13 times for the first team and was yet to score a goal. I just prayed that Gregg listened to the coaches and trusted their judgement.

I talked things over with my father: did I really want to be a footballer? Should I jump before I was pushed? My dad knew this wasn't how I really felt, and as we talked it became clear that I still wanted to forge a career in the professional game and that my ambition to play at the highest level was burning as brightly as ever.

This desire to remain a footballer was perhaps out of necessity as well as desire. The South Wales mining community was, as in the rest of the country, embroiled in a bitter industrial dispute with the government, and the whole future of the mining communities in the Valleys seemed quite precarious. With the general economic crisis (a 1970s version of the 'credit crunch') affecting the country, the option of going into a factory or down the mines was not one I could necessarily fall back on. I also doubted whether I would be accepted onto a teacher-training course. Places were much sought after, as teaching was at that time a highly competitive and well-regarded profession, and having turned down a place at Cardiff College the previous year I didn't think they would offer me another one.

It was with some trepidation that I opened the letter that summoned me down to the Vetch that close season. As I sat in the corridor waiting for my turn to see the manager, my mind whirred back to my performances the previous season, and each mistake and error I made came flooding back to me. My nerves weren't helped as a succession of the young lads passed me in tears after being told they were to be released. It also became known that some of the more established players were also being shown the door, such as Brian Evans and Dai Gwyther.

Nowadays, when clubs release young lads, a list is circulated to other teams and trial matches are arranged so they can impress other managers. Back then, it was very different. Once released, that was more or less the end of a player's dreams, and they would enter the local job market and begin a career in a local factory or, if they were lucky, gain a trade in one of the local heavy industries. Along with the end of their footballing aspirations, the dream of a big transfer to another club and the financial rewards that were slowly seeping into the game at the higher levels also came to an end.

When it was my turn to face the manager, I was racked with nerves, but thankfully Gregg offered me another contract. He told me that he was pleased with my progress and that if I knuckled down and worked hard, I had a future in the game. I walked out of the door still dreaming of becoming a full Welsh international, playing at the top level and earning a good living from the game.

My dreams were still intact, but I was soon brought down to earth with a bump, especially with regard to my ambitions of a wealthy lifestyle, as for most of the close seasons at the start of my career the other lads and I had to find summer work to make ends meet. Wyndham Evans and I both worked for Paul, a local builder. I painted and decorated, did the odd plastering job, and on one occasion laid the foundations for Harry Gregg's extension. Whilst Wyndham had served his apprenticeship as a tool maker in a car factory in Llanelli and could be described as useful, my DIY skills were at best useless. Whether Paul's customers turned a blind eye to my craftsmanship (or lack of it!) because I played for the Swans, I do not know. In fact, I would be surprised if he made a profit. Everything I put up instantly fell down, and using a spirit level proved to be an impossible task. Paul, to his credit, was a great boss and spent most of his working day talking to us about football.

In the 1950s and '60s, the brand of football at the Vetch – a pass-and-move style and high-scoring games carried out with a blend of local talent and players bought from other clubs to complement the indigenous talent – became known as the 'Swansea Way'. In the decades following the war, Swansea was a hotbed of football, with an endless supply of locally produced players. A list of names of players who played for the club at that time reads like a who's who of Welsh football and includes Cliff Jones, Terry Medwin, Ivor and Lennie Allchurch, Mel Charles, Mel Nurse, Barrie Jones, Barrie Hole and Herbie Williams, to name but a few, and with such players it was easy to see how this brand of attacking football could be achieved. By the time Roy Bentley arrived at the club in August 1969, this seam of riches had all but dried up, and the playing style changed, with an emphasis on a more physical and rugged approach to the game.

CURT

As the 1973–74 season approached under Harry Gregg, we all wondered if this physical style was to be continued. The first session proved that there was a distinct similarity between Gregg's and Bentley's training methods. Over the close season, Gregg had installed ex-Leeds and Juventus star John Charles as a coach to work alongside Harry and Roy. You can imagine the optimism amongst the lads when we saw Wales's greatest-ever footballer at the Vetch. But after the inevitable fitness training, our short-lived dreams were shattered, for it was back to the anything-and-everything-goes game behind the North Bank. It looked as if this robust style was now going to be the Swansea Way!

In one session, Big John climbed for a header, only to be challenged by a young apprentice named Terry Walsh, who with elbows leading knocked one of Charlo's teeth out. Luckily for Terry, John was known as the 'Gentle Giant', or 'Il Gigante Buono' as the Juventus fans nicknamed him, otherwise I am sure he would have snapped the now quivering trainee in two. John remarked afterwards that even in Italy, where cynical play was part and parcel of being a pro, he had never experienced training like that!

These sessions were a taster of what was to dominate under Gregg's stewardship of the club, and in all honesty this robust and physical approach to the game was not really my forte. His footballing philosophy was reinforced when he signed Mickey Evans from Walsall and Paul Bevan from Shrewsbury, as both players were big and uncompromising. Life in the bottom tier of English league football was, it seemed, going to be focused on fighting our way out of the division, sometimes almost literally.

There was one more positive at the start of the 1973–74 season when Herbie, a man who believed in playing football the Swansea Way, was appointed player-coach. But under Harry's regime, each game was a battle, and there was certainly not going to be too much of an emphasis on total football.

Brian Evans was a wonderfully gifted winger who signed from

Abergavenny Thursdays in 1963 and played 355 games for the Swans. He also represented Wales, which was no mean feat, as the national side had some great midfield players around that time, but Brian despaired at the team's approach. Gregg's tactics meant that both Brian and I were getting kicked all over the park. Even though we hadn't actually committed any fouls ourselves, it was obvious the other teams' players were exacting retribution on us because our teammates were kicking them. In fact, Brian left for Hereford soon after, perhaps because of the harsh treatment he received and Gregg's unwillingness to change tactics. I have to admit that if I had been a more established pro, I might have been tempted to look for another club as well.

In hindsight, perhaps Gregg did ultimately want us to play more attractive football, but results were paramount for a new manager. Even in those days, football management was a precarious occupation, and the industry was results driven. And some players, such as Wyndham, did thrive on the boss's style of play. On many occasions, he was thrust up front to 'roughen up' the opposing keeper or centre-half. In the dressing-room before the game, Harry would lay out his game plan: on the first corner, Paul, Mickey, Wyndham or all three were to let the keeper know they were there so he would think twice before coming out for another cross. In other words, they would smash into the goalkeeper and hammer him into the back of the net. A great ploy, except it sometimes took us over an hour to get our first corner!

In his first season, Harry Gregg certainly showed us who was the gaffer and his reputation in the game as being a hard man was reinforced. On one occasion, when we were playing Darlington, he had a touchline disagreement during the first half with their manager Peter Madden, a rugged, no-nonsense centre-half in his playing days. As the half-time whistle went, the dispute carried on up the tunnel and into the referee's room. The two managers chucked the officials out and had a fist fight as all the players looked on in amazement.

In another incident later that season, Gregg climbed over the perimeter fence at the Vetch to have a go at some away supporters who were giving us stick. And whilst he could mix it with the opposition and away fans, our own players could get it in the neck from him as well. During that period at the Vetch, supporters could buy pasties off sellers walking the perimeter track, much like buying an ice cream in the pictures. People from the back of the North Bank would pass their money to the front and, amazingly, the pasty would reach the buyer at the back of the terracing. When you think of some of the characters down the Vetch, it is incredible that nothing happened to the money or the food. During one match, to the great amusement of everybody except the Swans manager, Tony Millington, our goalie, decided to get a pasty, and as we were attacking he was leaning on the post eating away whilst talking to the *Evening Post* photographer Len Pitson. Gregg turned around, saw this and went crazy, screaming obscenities at Millie.

When he got to the dressing-room, Millie was lifted off his feet by his neck and told, in no uncertain terms, what a disgrace he was to his profession. Not that that deterred Millie, who was a real fans' favourite. He was seen swinging on his crossbar, waving to the crowd, many more times after that.

In another game, I think it was against Peterborough, one of the opposition players kicked the ball in temper into the old 'Double Decker' stand after an offside decision had gone against him. Unfortunately, the ball smashed into the face of a young lad, who was naturally very upset and burst into tears. Millie was so incensed, he ran over and punched the guilty player in the face. The next thing we knew, all 22 players were involved in a massive punch-up.

Millie was great to be around, and he was a very good keeper who played 21 times for Wales. Unfortunately, he was involved in a bad car crash in 1975 and was confined to a wheelchair, but this didn't stop him from helping Wrexham to improve conditions for disabled supporters. I was sad to hear in April 2009 that he was not in the best of health.

My first full season in the Fourth Division was hard work but even though the style of play didn't really suit me, I missed only a handful of games and appeared in both the League Cup and FA Cup, so I did feel as though I was slowly establishing myself as part of the first-team set-up. Even though I didn't think I fitted in with Gregg's style of play, I did, in fact, play thirty-eight league games during the 1973–74 season and scored the first four goals of my professional career.

At the start of the 1974–75 season, as a result of his connections, Gregg was able to attract the likes of Jimmy Rimmer from Man United on loan, which gave everyone connected with the club the idea that things could only get better. How wrong could we have been? The brand of football did not change, which meant crowds dwindled. Some of the players were not enthused by the tactics or lack of atmosphere, and we inevitably began a poor run of results, which included losing to non-league Kettering in the first round of the FA Cup and going out of the League Cup to Exeter.

Every day at training, there was an increasing sense that a change was imminent, and it finally happened midseason when Gregg left for Crewe. Whilst that did not come as a complete shock, I was surprised when Harry Griffiths was asked by the chairman, Malcolm Struel, to take over. I don't know if it was lack of money or better the devil you know, but it proved to be an inspired choice. The first thing Harry – Griffiths, not Gregg! Sorry for the confusion, but I was only twenty, and this was my third manager! – told us was that we were going back to the way football had always been played by the Swans.

For the rest of the season, we did attempt to play the Swansea Way, but time was against us, and we finished in the bottom four of the division, which meant we had to apply for re-election to the Football League. Unlike today, when there is automatic relegation to the Conference, those clubs at the bottom had to go cap in hand to a special meeting at which all the other clubs' chairmen would vote for or against the bottom four remaining in the league or a team from one of the many feeder leagues coming in. Luckily for us, there was, understandably, a closed-shop mentality, which meant that those at the bottom were inevitably re-elected, as we duly were. In the 1970s, any team, especially in the lower divisions, that voted for a club's removal from the Football League ran the risk that the decision would come back to haunt them if they ever found themselves in a similar position in the future.

After being saved by the other clubs from being thrown out of the league completely, the 1975–76 season seemed to offer the club, with the new manager now settled in, the chance to wipe the slate clean. The Swansea public were used to a certain standard and quality of play from their team, and our poor efforts over the previous seasons had seen the crowds dwindle to a record low of 2,050 on average. It was no great surprise that only 3,000 saw our first game of that campaign, a 1–1 draw with Tranmere, with Wyndham getting our goal.

During that period, my life off the field was changing, as I moved out of Harry and Gwen's to set up home with Pauline, although my surrogate family could still keep an eye on me, as we only moved next door. Pauline was a Rhondda girl who attended Porth County Girls School, and we got married in 1974.

I felt that Harry's appointment would be good news for me, as he had always been very supportive of my career, and I think he knew as much about me as I knew about myself. Harry was given a mandate by the chairman to achieve success but with a brand of football that was more in keeping with the style demanded by the Swansea fans. I think Harry was not only deeply hurt with us having had to go cap in hand to the other clubs' chairmen to save our league status, but also with the style of play that had got us into that position in the first place. He argued it was time to bring the ball down and to bring back the pass-and-move style of past Swans teams.

The emphasis on this brand of football was drummed into us during the close season, which was music to my ears. Harry also made a very astute signing, with the acquisition of George Smith from Cardiff. George had played at the very top with Birmingham City and was brought in to help nurture the youngsters, who were starting to come through the youth and reserve teams.

I would argue that Harry Griffiths very much laid the foundations of our later success and should be given far more credit for his role in the rehabilitation of the club. We still had the backbone of the side that could compete with the more physical teams in the league, but flair players were also given more of a free rein and encouraged to express themselves. Training became more fun, and although crowds were still relatively disappointing I think the spectators who did regularly come through the turnstiles were appreciative of our efforts.

In September 1973, I scored the first goal of my professional career at Torquay's Plainmoor ground, and it was the same venue during the 1975–76 season that marked what I believe to be one of the defining moments of my career. I can't remember why (perhaps there were some injuries), but on the morning of the game Harry informed me that he had decided he was going to give me a run out in a more advanced central position. When I look back, I wonder if fate played a hand, because shortly before this the Swans had taken a player by the name of Tommy Tynan on loan only to release him after a month. Tommy later went on to score goals for fun, netting over 250 in a successful career with Newport County and Plymouth Argyle, amongst others. If the Swans had kept him, I would have probably remained out wide or in a deeper position. To borrow a phrase, 'Football is a funny old game.'

That day, I played in a freer role alongside Gary Moore, and from then on the goals came more regularly for me. I ended up playing in forty-one matches and netting nine times that season. Because of our improved performances, finishing a more respectable 11th in the division, we were a little disappointed that the Swansea public didn't come out in bigger numbers, and it was a little embarrassing when the last home game of the season, a 2–2 draw with Brentford, was watched by a record low Vetch attendance of only 1,311 fans. We did reach the final of the Welsh Cup, but this turned out to be little consolation, as we ended up losing 3–0 to Cardiff in front of a crowd of over 10,000 at the Vetch.

Ever the optimist, I felt a real buzz as the 1976–77 season approached, and a significant change seemed to be taking place at the club, as the coaching staff were actively encouraging the development of more home-grown talent – perhaps not to the extent seen in the decades after the Second World War, but a promising crop nonetheless. Joining Wyndham, Robbie and me in the first team was Jeremy Charles, son of Mel and nephew of John. I knew what it was like to be the nephew of a famous footballer trying to make his way in the game, so I got on well with Charlo and tried to offer the wisdom of my albeit limited experience. Two goals on his debut against Newport County went some way to allaying any fears that he or the coaching staff might have had about whether he could carry the inevitable pressure associated with the Charles name. After leaving the Swans, he played and scored in the League Cup final of 1986 for Oxford United at Wembley, ironically against Robbie's QPR.

Charlo was great to have around the dressing-room and was the club organiser, getting the lads together for a few beers or family get-togethers. Since retiring from the game, he has gone into the hospitality side of things, arranging anything from a weekend break to tickets for Champions League ties or Joe Calzaghe fights. Perhaps his career in the entertainment business was inspired by his role as the team's social secretary during his playing days. We were in Magaluf one year, and Charlo, as ever, was in charge of the drinks kitty. He confidently strolled up to the bar to get a round in and said, 'I will have six bottles of beer for the lads and a Bacardi and Coke on the rocks for me, please, barman. And no ice!'

Charlo now tells me he is an IT specialist, but I have since found out that this amounts to him being able to switch a computer on and off! He might have been an even greater player if not for the mystery illnesses that affected him. If you look through the record books, they will show that he was often unwell over the Christmas period!

Of all the players at that time, it was probably me, Robbie and Charlo who were closest. When Roberto Martínez signed for Wigan with two of his Spanish compatriots, they were dubbed the 'Three Amigos' by the media. We had that nickname in Swansea years before. Not because of our sultry Latin looks – not Robbie, anyway – but because of our close-season activities. Or should I say the activities of some quick-thinking Swansea lads on holiday. For a couple of years, when we arrived back for pre-season, there were letters from various girls thanking us for the great time they'd had in Spain and asking if it would be OK to come and see us play. Can you imagine the shock on their faces when we met them with their tickets? They had been duped by three lads imitating us on the Costas! We've never found out the identities of those lads.

Also coming onto the scene around that time was a promising defender from the Port Tennant area by the name of Nigel Stevenson. 'Speedy' was a big affable lad, who would do anything for anyone, and he was a great mate. Unfortunately, he was also accident prone and could sometimes lose it. If there were any mishaps, Speedy was invariably involved. For example, there was the time when he decided to have treatment on a leg injury. He had to put his foot into a hot wax bath and take it out again quickly. Unfortunately for Speedy, he left his foot in for too long and suffered third-degree burns. The pain was so excruciating that he jumped up and knocked himself out on a low beam in the treatment room!

When a club encourages home-grown talent, there seems to be an increased bond between the fans and players. This can sometimes put extra pressure on the local lads when things are not going so well. Swansea is more like a village than a town – everybody knows everyone, and there are not many well-kept secrets! – so we had to be very careful not to criticise other players in public, and we would really look out for each other. We were developing a real sense of camaraderie, and I think a successful club can thrive on such a strong bond amongst the players. Those drafted in became part of the 'family', and after a game on a Saturday night you would sometimes find the whole squad out with their partners for a few pints and a meal. We made a real effort to fit in and were never flash or arrogant, and I think that also endeared us to the fans.

This spirit was fostered by Harry, who as I keep mentioning had very strong feelings about the club and the town – or city as it had now become. He wanted us to have a local identity, which I feel is sometimes missing today, with all the foreign imports in football. However, I have to say that Roberto Martínez tried to infuse the 'Jack' culture in his signings, and that is why the people of Swansea accepted the players he brought in as their own, as I suppose they did with me!

During the early games of the new season, my more advanced role continued, and in many home games I was playing virtually as a centre-forward. I did not have to track back so much and certainly not man-mark an opposing player like I was instructed to by Gregg. He wanted me to offload the ball as quickly as possible, whereas Harry Griffiths knew my strengths and encouraged me to take people on. After five years on the Vetch Field books, I was an ever-present for the first time, playing in all 46 league games. We had some memorable matches that season, such as when we were 4–0 down with 20 minutes to go at home to Stockport in March only to come back to draw 4–4. As a professional, it was not what you wanted, but the fans seemed to love it, and the crowds steadily began to improve, which was probably helped by the fact that we were the division's top scorers, banging in 92 goals, of which I contributed 14, my best return to date.

After beating Newport 3–1 at home in early April, we went on a fantastic unbeaten run, winning seven and drawing two of our next nine games. We faced Watford at home in the penultimate game of the season and were red-hot favourites to continue our excellent unbeaten run and snatch a dramatic promotion. I don't know if it was the pressure or the realisation that we could actually do it, but we simply didn't turn up on the night and lost 4–1. This was even more frustrating when we travelled to champions Cambridge United for the last game of the season and beat them 3–2, taking their unbeaten home record in the process. We eventually lost out to Bradford City on the final promotion place by a single point, as they had a better goal difference by three. If we had drawn against Watford, the fact that we had scored far more goals than them would have seen us promoted. Once again, the cup competitions proved to be a disaster, with first-round knockouts in both, an embarrassing home defeat to non-league Minehead in the FA Cup and a 5–1 hammering by Bolton in the League Cup.

My improving performances attracted the attention of the Welsh selectors, and I made my only appearance for the Under-23s when I came on as a sub against the Scots. In the same period, I also played for the Under-21s against England.

With hindsight, that season was a defining one, despite narrowly missing out on promotion. In his first full season as manager, Harry was inspirational, and a lot of credit must also go to the chairman for his bold, if somewhat forced, appointment. I sometimes wonder if Harry would have had the job if finances were not so perilous. Conversely, what sort of job would Harry have done if he'd had a few bob to spend?

When we were not playing, we would sometimes go down to St Helen's to watch the rugby. That Easter, we all went to watch the annual match between Swansea RFC and the Barbarians, and I seemed to spend the entire match discussing the improved fortunes of the Swans with other members of the crowd. The general feeling was that Harry's insistence on returning to the Swansea Way was increasingly galvanising the fans behind the team. He had put us on a strong footing for the following season's campaign, and there seemed to be a much greater enthusiasm around the city about the team's performances.

It was, therefore, with renewed optimism that we approached the 1977–78 season, and everyone was quietly confident that Harry was going to help us launch a successful assault on promotion, which would hopefully lead us back to at least the old Second Division, where he always maintained the Swans rightly belonged and where, apart from Rotherham United, they had historically spent the greatest amount of time.

As a result of what Harry had achieved the previous season, we entered the campaign as one of the bookies' favourites for promotion, but things did not go according to plan. For the first half of the season, we played fairly consistently, and a 4–0 away win at Hartlepool on New Year's Eve put us seventh in the league. Although we had some very good results during that period, the game that stands out for me was on Saturday, 12 November at the Vetch. We were comfortably beating Crewe 2–0 about twenty minutes into the second half when, in what I can only describe as an indescribable five minutes, I scored a hat-trick. For that performance, I received the match ball and 12 bottles of whisky.

My football career was brought into perspective when Pauline was rushed into hospital with a clot on the brain. The club were extremely supportive and left the decision to play or not with me. I decided that I would combine playing with travelling to Llwynypia Hospital in the Rhondda.

As a consequence of our mixed bag of results, Harry was relieved of his duties in October and reinstated a month later, and, despite our good form, by the turn of 1978 he was again under pressure. The old Swansea gossip mill was in gear once more, with talk of yet another possible managerial change. Quite a few people were being mentioned as possible replacements, including Colin Addison, Eddie McCreadie and John Toshack. Tosh looked to be on his way out of Liverpool, but he had failed a medical with Leicester City, a thigh injury preventing the move.

The rumours were gathering apace, and at a Welsh get-together I asked him if they were true. He dismissed them out of hand, and as he had no coaching experience it seemed the rumours were both far-fetched and unfounded. A few days later, Wyndham, Robbie, Charlo and I were strolling around town when we spotted Tosh. He came over and once again denied that he was in the frame for the manager's job, telling us he was there for a sporting function. Yet within 48 hours, on St David's Day 1978, it was announced that he was the next manager in the Swans' turbulent history.

John had won almost every honour in the game with Liverpool, both domestically and in Europe, before he joined Fourth Division Swansea City. From a packed hero-worshipping Anfield, Tosh now arrived at a club whose crowds were improving but rarely rose above five figures. A household name had decided at the age of only 28, without any management experience or formal coaching qualifications, to step down to the bottom rung of the English game.

Whilst we were all incredulous, it is worth noting that Tosh is no fool, something that has been proved time and time again as the seasons have passed by. He had done his homework on the squad, seen what Harry had achieved and listened to the promises of Malcolm Struel. I believe it was the nucleus of youngsters, the young talent that was available to him, that swayed him. The local talent coming through was a bonus, and Tosh was not afraid to give youth its head, as he has proved as Wales manager.

The whole city seemed to be talking about Tosh's appointment, and we were bubbling with anticipation, wondering how far he could take us. Amid all the euphoria, though, we perhaps forgot one important person: Harry Griffiths. Did the board think he had taken the club as far as he could? Looking back, I think Harry could have taken us further. At the time, though, I think we were all caught up in the excitement of the moment and maybe forgot Harry and his feelings for a little while. He must have been really hurting, but it was the mark of the man that he put his feelings to one side and was prepared to remain at the club as Tosh's assistant. For Harry, the club was paramount, and if he could help in any way, he would.

Tosh's first game was home to Watford on 3 March 1978, and a crowd of over 15,000 turned up to watch a thrilling 3–3 draw under the Friday-night floodlights. Nothing had changed playing-wise, as we were still banging them in, but also conceding them as well. The team that night, with the exception of Tosh, was Harry's team. He had brought on the youngsters and supplemented them with astute signings. As far as the fans were concerned, however, the appointment of John Toshack would give the team the extra boost that they needed to secure promotion. A record 8–0 home victory over Hartlepool in early April, in which both Robbie and I scored hat-tricks, seemed to be firm evidence of this. After Hartlepool, we beat Southport 3–0 at home, which meant we had taken 14 points from the previous 18 available. We then suffered a setback at Crewe, which probably delighted their manager, Harry Gregg. After beating Burnley three days later, their manager, Jim Iley, proclaimed that we were the best side his team had faced that season. Next up were Grimsby, who beat us 2–1, which meant that we only had a three-point cushion from the chasing pack. It was still nip and tuck, but we were in a better position than the previous season when we'd been chasing fourth spot. At least now we were looking down at the rest.

With promotion to the Third Division in sight and with two home games left, confidence was high. As we gathered in the dressing-room to prepare for the first of them against Scunthorpe on Tuesday, 25 April 1978, there was a commotion in the treatment room. A few of the lads rushed in to find Harry on the floor. He had collapsed and died of a heart attack. Some of the lads were in shock, as they had seen Harry and had come to tell the rest of us the news. Thankfully,

I didn't witness it, because I always want to remember Harry's face with a smile on it.

As you can imagine, we were all dumbstruck, so my recollection of the rest of the day's events is a little unclear. I do remember Wyndham getting up, walking out of the ground and going down to the beach to be on his own and gather his thoughts. Unfortunately, we still had a game to play that night. I suppose the club could have contacted the Football League for a postponement, but instead they contacted Gwen, who said the match should go ahead. This perhaps helped to take our minds temporarily off what had happened, and we could play and win the game for Harry. In a surreal atmosphere, we won 3–1, but there was no cause for celebration, even though we had almost certainly sealed our promotion to Division Three.

We were determined to ensure we gained promotion as a tribute to Harry's memory and did so the following Saturday by beating Halifax 2–0 at a packed Vetch. It was Harry who had laid the foundations for our success, and we celebrated promotion and his life after the game. Despite having won promotion and equalling Cyril Pearce's club record of 32 league goals in a season, these achievements were tinged with sadness. His passing had a massive effect on me, as I was particularly close to Harry and Gwen. I will be for ever grateful to him for helping me achieve what I did in the game. Swansea football club was Harry's life, so I guess if he had been able to choose where to die it would have been his beloved Vetch Field.

Harry was a true legend, and a bar at the ground was named in his honour. It's a funny thing in football, but we only commemorate someone's contribution after they have gone; for example, Ivor's statue and Robbie's bust at the Liberty Stadium. It's a pity we do not celebrate people's achievements when they are still with us. Having said that, it would be a fitting tribute to one of Swansea's favourite sons to be remembered at the new stadium, with perhaps a more high-profile memorial, as it might all have been so different without Harry Griffiths.

CURT

By the end of the 1977–78 season, the roller-coaster journey that would take the club to the heights of the top of the First Division table and all the way back to the bottom tier in the space of only seven years had begun!

4

TOSH

Since my debut in 1972, I had seen a string of well-known managers and coaches come through the revolving doors at Swansea, including Roy Bentley, Harry Gregg, Harry Griffiths, Roy Saunders, Herbie Williams and John Charles. Off the field, the club faced mounting debts, forcing the chairman to sell the ground to the council for a knockdown price of £50,000, with a grant of £150,000 to help with the overdraft. I wonder if councils today would be able or allowed to bail out the many clubs who have accumulated millions of pounds worth of debt.

I was happy, however, with the way my own career was developing by 1978 and was now a regular in the Welsh squad. I was also very proud that the previous season I was voted divisional Player of the Year by the managers of the other Fourth Division teams. During this period, the chairman and the board had also turned down a substantial six-figure bid, rumoured to be £165,000, for me from Sunderland in the months leading up to Tosh's appointment. It seemed there was a growing chance that I would now achieve my long-time ambition of playing in the top flight. I just hoped that Tosh could help make it happen with the Swans.

Even though his playing career was being increasingly hampered by injuries, there were still quite a few clubs chasing Tosh's signature from all four divisions of the Football League, as well as one or two, such as Anderlecht, on the Continent. Along with Tommy Smith, he also turned down the chance to manage Hereford United, saying that he wanted to come home to Wales. There were rumours linking him to his home-town club, but, like the Swans, Cardiff were in financial trouble. Tosh's purported wages of £400 a week at Liverpool also probably frightened many suitors off.

It could be argued that the Swans were guilty of tapping Tosh up. Malcolm Struel had been given a tip-off from a guy organising a corporate event that Tosh was in town. The chairman turned up at The Dragon Hotel, the venue for the event, and drove Tosh to his home, believing the press would get wind of it if they met in a hotel. One of Malcolm's strongest allies on the board, Tom Phillips, joined them on the Sunday, and the club's vision was outlined. A gentleman's agreement was put in place, but Liverpool had not actually given permission for the talks, and the deal also had to be ratified by the board.

Another obstacle was Harry Griffiths, who had dedicated his life to the club. Tosh was told that if there was no job for Harry, then there was no job for him either. The chairman then had the unenviable task of turning up at Harry's home to break the news, a task made more difficult by the fact that the chairman, manager and their families had become very good friends. Harry was no one's fool, so I guess he knew what was coming when Malcolm put his arm around him that Sunday evening. Lots of people thought the club had stabbed Harry in the back, but he was included in the events leading up to Tosh's appointment, including meeting the Liverpool board at Anfield, where their chairman, John Smith, gave his blessing to the appointment. A month into Tosh's reign, Harry declared that these were the happiest days of his footballing life.

Just like David Goldstone, the previous chairman, Malcolm Struel was first and foremost a Swans fan. When I first started off in the

Combination side, I remember Mr Goldstone watching us at one of the London grounds. After the game, he went over to one of the coaching staff and demanded the reimbursement of his Tube fare in cash, probably only a couple of pence in those days, even though he was a London-based solicitor. This probably explains why he came to own such a large portfolio of property and real estate, including Lands End.

Struel had his critics over the years, especially when things were not going too well, but he had a grand plan for the Swans. He used to walk around town telling everyone who would listen that there was no reason why we could not reach the First Division. Even though he was a fan, there was many a time when he could have walked away, especially as many people openly ridiculed his ambitions for the club. There were times in the dark days when his car was covered in acid or the windows of his business smashed. I guess he tried to run the club as he did his company, but football is not like any other business, so there were times when his heart might have ruled his head. Like the time he bought the goalkeeper Tony Belotti with his own money.

Since Noel Dwyer's days, Swansea seemed to have become somewhat of a goalkeepers' graveyard, with many coming and going without much success. Malcolm was also personally responsible for bringing in Tony Millington when the manager was on holiday. Roy Bentley was furious when he returned. 'Mal, what have you done?' I remember him asking. Millie was two stone overweight and had a reputation for being a bad trainer. Perhaps that was one of the reasons he signed him, as Malcolm used to join us a couple of times a week on the run from the Mumbles, and for the first few weeks of pre-season he used to come in ahead of Millie, Barrie Hole and Geoff Thomas. On one occasion, Barrie and Geoff did beat the chairman, but the manager was not happy when he caught them getting out of a furniture van, having a fag. In fairness to Millie, he trained hard, lost the weight and produced performances that got him into the Wales squad.

Malcolm joined the board as chief executive in 1969 as Goldstone's representative. When he eventually took over as chairman in 1972, he outlined his vision to reach the summit of the football pyramid. I guess he saw something in Tosh that could match his own ambitions. It was a shrewd bit of business, because he had tried to sign Tosh as a player on a few occasions but had been scared off by the £80,000 price tag. Now he had negotiated for Tosh to join us as player-manager on a free. However, Liverpool did have a sell-on clause, and they also had first refusal on any Swans players who were transfer-listed.

It was a miracle that Malcolm lured someone with Tosh's pedigree to the Vetch, because in footballing terms we were near the end of the line. We had never had a rich benefactor, which meant we were undercapitalised, which in turn limited the type of player who could be attracted and had an impact on the size of the crowd. To get a player such as Tosh, the chairman had to pay a premium, which meant he was open to criticism for overspending. In reality, though, we were always at the bottom of the salary league when compared with most other clubs. Even during our two seasons in the First Division in the early 1980s, we were in the bottom three where wage expenditure was concerned. I remember Robbie asking the chairman, tongue in cheek, during that period if he thought it right that he should be marking someone on five times the wages that he was getting.

At the end of the day, though, we all thought that our wages were reasonable. We played because of our love of the Swans, not monetary gain. The ordinary man in the street, who paid our wages, felt the brunt of a number of recessions during my time at the club. To a degree, we were inflation proof, as we signed contracts that were not affected by economic downturn, so we never rocked the boat. It is a pity that some of the players today do not share a little of our philosophy!

Tosh had initially run the rule over us in late February 1978 away to Rochdale, who were bottom of the league and had not won a game since the last week of December. He was accompanied by his long-time friend and teammate Emlyn Hughes, who later told me that he tried to talk Tosh out of taking the job, partly due to the fact that we lost that game 2–1. Tosh, however, was not and is not a man for turning. He had seen enough that night to convince him that the time was right to step into management, despite our poor performance. Compared with his Liverpool and Wales days, the Swans would be a completely different experience. We certainly had youngsters who could play, and we were a free-scoring team, even if we did concede the odd few!

Tosh was going to be the highest-paid player-manager in the country, with total control of the playing staff. However, at the last moment, he had been invited to an interview with Cardiff, which went very well – so well that they offered him the post of assistant manager. Tosh thought that he was being interviewed for the number-one job. I would have loved to have been a fly on the wall when he realised. Still, Cardiff's loss was our gain!

As players, we faced a dilemma with the new appointment, as some of us knew Tosh from the international scene. Did we call him 'Boss', 'Gaffer', 'John' or 'Tosh'? Pat Lally provided the answer. He left the welcome meeting and came back in with a chair with the word 'Bosh' written on it, although we did call him other names over the coming years – out of earshot, of course!

Before his first match in charge, Tosh called the whole squad together and outlined his vision for the club, telling us that within four years we would be in the First Division. We were incredulous. I knew that he had taken a good look at us, but the First? I looked across to Wyndham, who looked baffled and bemused. And if Mr Swansea City could not believe what he was hearing, what chance did the rest of us have?

Wyndham, the consummate pro, was the one player Tosh needed on his side. He epitomised everything that the club was about. He could run faster, was stronger and harder, and could drink more than anyone else! If Wyndham was injured, he would get on the physio's bench and through gritted teeth convince everyone that he was fit. In those days, if you were injured you missed the bonuses that were on offer, so there was many a time that Wyndham would play through the pain barrier, as he had a family to support. Charlo could have taken a leaf out of Wyndham's book. He had a reputation for being slightly injury prone, and while he was having treatment Wyndham would lead the lads singing, 'Eight days a month. You only work eight days a month!'

If Harry Griffiths turning me into a striker was the main reason for my success, then Wyndham ran him a close second. I had to face him every day in training, and if I could survive his tackles, I could face anything the rest of the Football League had to offer. To be a success in the professional game, you have to have an edge to your game. I might have been considered a flair player, but Wyndham most certainly helped me develop the hardness that was necessary to succeed as a pro and to ensure that no one messed with me! Both of us had entered the game later than usual, me to finish my education, Wyndham to finish his apprenticeship as a toolmaker, although Wyndham had been offered a contract with Stoke City when he left school after he appeared alongside John 'Josh' Mahoney in a few reserve games. Unfortunately, he got homesick so returned to Llanelli.

As late starters, we were spared the humiliation of some of the pranks that are played on football apprentices, although we did play a few ourselves. Like the time we told one of the kids that Tosh wanted the posts and crossbars cleaned before a game. You can guess what followed after we hid all the stepladders. A young boy was crawling along the crossbar with a damp cloth. Another time, Tosh ordered the club to put carpet tiles in the dressing-room instead of wood flooring. Within hours, Wyndham had told the kids that Tosh wanted the tiles cleaned and disinfected. By the time Tosh got in, the carpets were ruined.

I did not have many pranks played on me, but I do remember my first couple of months acquainting myself with the city. Wyndham would grab my hand whenever we were crossing the Kingsway, telling everyone I needed help to cross the road, as I had never seen a dual carriageway in the Rhondda!

The first few games of Tosh's reign didn't produce much difference in performances from what had gone on before, as we won a few but also lost matches when perhaps we should not have. I think it was after our record-breaking 8–0 win over Hartlepool a month after he took over as manager that we began to realise that even though he was only 28 Tosh had something special about him. He had certainly brought an extra degree of professionalism to the club, and we were experiencing things for the first time. There weren't any cliques, but some lads did socialise together more than others; for example, Speedy, Charlo, Robbie, Wyndham and me. This continued, but after training we all had to eat together – not a lavish affair in one of the hotels, but beans on toast in Dolly's Nest under the Centre Stand. He would also take us away for a few days midweek; for example, after the Hartlepool game we went to watch the Liverpool derby as the guests of Everton, whilst earlier in the day we had visited Aintree to have our photos taken with Red Rum. Tosh was rewarding us and at the same time encouraging us to feel like we were achieving something in the game.

We would also use Liverpool's Melwood training facilities from time to time, and Bill Shankly and Bob Paisley would involve themselves in these sessions. We picked up some good habits and tried things that we had never done before. One thing that was impressed on us was that there were to be no stars – we were a collective. When we watched Liverpool train, the first team would have shooting practice and the apprentices would fetch the wayward balls. Then they would swap and household names would retrieve the balls for the kids. Those were the values that the new manager instilled in the squad.

Tosh was also a master of psychology and mind games, anything to help us raise our performance. One of the first things he did on arriving at the club was place a notice in the dressing-room. It said that there was to be an end-of-season trip to Majorca but that there were only 18 seats on the plane. Whoever had the most Man of the Match performances would be first on, followed by the next best until the seats were taken. Every game became more competitive, and the players had to nominate each match's winner. If Wyndham gave away a penalty, the rest of us would shout over that he would be taking his holidays on the Gower, or if I managed to score, it would be, 'Curt, get your passport!'

I did say he was into sports psychology, didn't I? We did not realise it – typical footballers, I suppose – but there were only 17 or so of us in the squad, which meant we were all going regardless of our performances. This psychology was not only for our benefit. Tosh would try to use it any way he could to get an advantage over the opposition.

Tosh, probably because of the way he played the game himself, liked to attempt aerial domination of other teams. That is not to detract from the way we played under him, as he also encouraged us to pass and move, but he definitely liked us to dominate in the air. That is why I think he rated Charlo so much, as he saw something of himself in him. King John was Tosh's hero, and he would forever be shouting in training to head the ball back from where it came.

Before a game, we would take a walk around the pitch, and Tosh would get all of the tall players together. If the opposing keeper or one of the centre-halves was shorter than us, Tosh would walk over with the rest and ask him how he was and if he was looking forward to the game. That was OK if you were six feet or more, but the likes of Gilo had to stay in the dressing-room until kick-off! I was all right, because with my 1970s haircut and platform shoes I looked about six feet ten!

All these positive changes and the combined efforts of Harry and Tosh helped us to gain promotion to the Third Division at the end of the 1977–78 season. Even though they were their own men, there were lots of similarities between Tosh and Harry, especially being masters of the put down. I remember one time when Wyndham was dropped. He confronted Harry, demanding to know why he was in the second team. 'Because we have not got a thirds, son,' was his reply.

Tosh would tell everyone what a good player they were, but face to face he would remind them of a chance they'd missed or something else they'd not done to his liking. What you saw with Tosh, though, was what you got. He alienated many with his directness, but I think he was a top manager. He was certainly a man of his word: a couple of months after his inaugural speech, we had completed part one of his four-year plan. Perhaps we were wrong to have had doubts. Or, more to the point, Wyndham's initial doubts had proved to be unfounded.

In the close season, Tosh approached the chairman about the size of the squad, which he believed needed strengthening, as we had only seventeen full-time pros and six apprentices. With Eddie May and Les Chappell retiring to focus on youth development, we were thin on the ground player-wise. I do not know how Eddie managed to get that job, as he could be another wind-up merchant. I remember the time Nigel Darling, another local lad, was introduced to the team before making his first-team debut, making him the youngest player in the club's history. After the introductions, Eddie turned to Harry and said, 'Bloody hell, Harry. I didn't know we had a policy of signing midgets now!' Even though he gave away about six stone and a foot advantage, Nigel flew at Eddie, and the rest of us had to break up the fight.

This episode reminds me of another mismatch earlier in my career. We were in the middle of a cold snap that meant we could not train at the Vetch, so we went for a run on the beach. On the way back, we called into a local boxing gym. Harry liked his pranks, so he organised a boxing competition amongst the squad: three-minute bouts, with the winners progressing to the next round. I can't remember the overall victor – probably Wyndham – but I do remember that the players insisted that Harry get the staff to fight as well. Harry was having none of it, because he was the manager. He did, however, convince King John and Roy Saunders to get into the ring together. When John stripped off, he had the physique of an Adonis; the same could not be said of Roy in his white vest. John told us he was once the heavyweight champion of his army unit, whilst Roy proclaimed he was the 'gnatweight' champion of his division.

Whilst the rest of us were in hysterics, they went at it hammer and tongs for three minutes. It was like watching *Tom and Jerry*. Roy was dancing around jabbing, whilst John was just trying to land a quick knockout punch. With both men still standing at the bell – or, rather, with Roy still standing – it went to the judges (me and Wyndham), resulting in an unanimous win on points for Roy.

If nothing else, Roy was a fierce competitor and did not like losing. He played local-league cricket well into retirement, and when he was old enough his son Dean played in the same side. If he was batting and he nicked one to the wicket-keeper, Roy would hold his ground, and a bowler had no chance with an lbw decision. On one occasion, Roy had his middle stump knocked out but still would not walk. 'What are you doing, Dad?' Dean asked. 'Take a look behind you. The middle stump is missing!'

Roy, holding his ground, turned and waved his bat at the umpire. 'If he had not given me the wrong guard, I would still be in!'

'Benny' was a great all-round sportsman, whether it be football, cricket or snooker. He enjoyed them all, and he gave a lot of his free time to support teams in the local kids' leagues. He will be sadly missed, especially by those of us who were lucky enough to be involved in the game with him. One thing is for sure: along with Harry, they have a great coaching team up there!

That summer, my contract came to an end, and I decided that I wanted to sample a higher level of football, even though we had been promoted to the Third Division. I felt I had made progress with Wales and was ready for a step up in league football. Also, lots of clubs had been showing an interest in me over the previous two seasons, including Crystal Palace, who had offered the Swans £160,000 for my services, although this was dismissed out of hand. I had talks with Tosh, and he reminded me that I had said 12 months earlier that I would only go if we failed to win promotion. He offered me a two-year deal that would probably have made me the highest-paid player in the lower divisions and reminded me that the Swans had given me a loyalty bonus the previous year, which had allowed me and Pauline to move from a flat to a house. I think this was worth about 20 grand a year, not a bad wage in those days, especially when you compared it with the average earned by many of the fans. As the talks progressed, Tosh realised it was not money but professional development that was important to me.

I think Tosh and the chairman reflected on my feelings over the next couple of days and decided a different approach was needed. The manager sat me down and told me he believed I was as important to the Swans as Kevin Keegan had been to Liverpool. One thing he was good at was making us believe in ourselves, and here he was comparing me to one of the game's greats. He told me he was strengthening both the playing side of things and the backroom staff. He was signing Alan 'Willy' Waddle, an old teammate from Liverpool, for £20,000 and bringing in Terry Medwin as assistant manager. Terry had been a coach at Cardiff when Tosh had started out and had also coached Norwich, Fulham and Wales. He was a much-respected figure in the game and demonstrated that Tosh was going to stick to his pass-and-move philosophy.

Tosh, like many of his predecessors, was unhappy with the goalkeeping position, which was understandable, as he had played with Ray Clemence at Liverpool and Gary Sprake with Wales. Tosh signed Geoff Crudgington, who had demonstrated his qualities in some fine displays against us for Crewe, breaking the Swans' transfer record for a keeper when he paid £25,000 to secure Geoff's services. Tosh was beginning to convince me that something special was happening and perhaps I was being too hasty in thinking about leaving. Then he threw something else into the mix, saying that he wanted to make me captain.

Unlike today, when some managers and clubs conduct their business through the media, Tosh was old school. Anything he said or did was kept in-house. Seeing I was still undecided, he could have told me something that would certainly have given me food for thought. 'It does not go out of this office,' I would have liked him to have said. 'But I've got two players in mind that I think will demonstrate to you that I mean business.' Tosh, however, was very single-minded. If I wanted to re-sign, all well and good, but he said it was down to me to make my own decision.

A week or so later, Tosh did reveal the potential new signings to the squad. We sat there in disbelief as he told us that Liverpool and England legends Tommy Smith and Ian Callaghan were probably going to sign. Both had won everything on offer at home and abroad and had been in the European Cup-winning squad the previous season, with Smithy missing out in the final because of injury, although he had scored in an earlier final. Liverpool had released them without a fee as a reward for their years of loyalty, and both had been playing in the States, Smithy with Los Angeles Aztecs and Cally with Fort Lauderdale. One season they were winning the game's highest honours, the next they were going to be plying their trade down the Vetch. I would be mad to go now, wouldn't I?

As the new season approached, the old revolving door was in full swing again, with the obligatory comings and goings. Out went Eddie May to coach Leicester, Keith Barber moved to Luton, Pat Lally to Doncaster and Mickey Conway, who had been badly injured in a car crash, finally admitted defeat in his battle to save his career. Smithy had signed, as had Phil Boersma, whilst Tosh was sweating on Cally, as First Division QPR had offered him a contract. He needn't have worried, however, as Cally had given his word, and in those days a player's promise meant something. After a couple of weeks' delay, the midfielder was on board for the next leg of Tosh's remarkable journey, signing a two-year contract.

There was a downside to the new signings: Tosh had relieved me of the playing captaincy, with Smithy taking over, although I was made club captain. Tommy made his debut against Lincoln City, and as we sat in the dressing-room beforehand I guess we could have been forgiven for feeling some pangs of jealousy. It was rumoured that he had been paid a signing-on fee of ten grand, which could have bought a nice little semi in 1978, and that he was on double our weekly wage. The opposite was true, though, as we reckoned that someone who had played over 500 games at the very top was going to help us develop as players.

Smithy's impact was immediate, not just on the park but in terms of bringing us better luck in the League Cup draw. For years, we had more often than not drawn (and lost to) other lower-league teams. This time when the draw was made we were paired against my boyhood heroes Tottenham Hotspur. I was really looking forward to the occasion, especially as they had just signed the Argentinian World Cup-winners Ossie Ardiles and Ricky Villa.

The arrival of the two former Liverpool stars had created a real buzz around the city, with season-ticket sales up and 25,000 fans paying record receipts to see the Spurs tie at the Vetch. Training was a pleasure, and Smithy had introduced another level of professionalism. You do not play that many games in the most competitive league in the world without doing something right.

However, it was not only the level of professionalism that he wanted to change. After a couple of games and training sessions, he gave his verdict on Wyndham. For years, managers, coaches and players had tried to tell Wyndham that he needed to calm down. He had been advised to stop clattering opposing wingers over the wall that ran the length of the North Bank and not to be too hasty with his challenges in the box. After about two weeks, Smithy turned to Wyndham in the dressing-room and offered his appraisal. 'Son, you have got to be nastier. You are too nice.' I knew Tommy had a reputation, but we were all wondering just how hard a player he was if he thought Wyndham was soft.

We beat Lincoln 3–0 in front of 17,000 fans, and although I scored I also picked up a knock that kept me out of the next game, a 2–2 draw away at Colchester. As a result, I spent the days leading up to the Spurs game in the treatment room, telling the physio I would have to play, even in a wheelchair – no way was I missing that one!

I did pass my fitness test and on the day of the match made my way to the ground through hundreds of fans who had not had the chance to see this level of opposition for years. The players went out onto the pitch before kick-off to sample the atmosphere and then made our way in for Tosh's team talk. As we were going through our individual pre-match customs, we sensed that Smithy was becoming increasingly agitated. We thought perhaps this was part of his routine until Wyndham asked him if he was OK. We were stunned by his response. 'Wyndham, this has got to stop before it gets out of hand, and I am the one who is going to stop it!' We all asked him what it was that was making him so incensed. 'These fucking foreigners. They are coming over in droves. If it does not stop, they will be taking our jobs!'

With hindsight, it seems that Smithy was quite perceptive in identifying the debate that still rages about whether there are too many foreign players in the British game. In a political sense, he also predated Gordon Brown's controversial comment about 'British jobs for British workers' by almost 30 years. It was a bit ironic, though, as the Swans were the first British club in the early 1970s to employ a European footballer under Common Market rules when Dutch keeper Nico Schroeder signed for the club.

As the game was about to start, we all took our usual positions for Spurs' kick-off except for Smithy. We all expected the usual ploy, involving the striker knocking the ball back to someone in the midfield who would then launch it towards the corner flag, where one of the back four would clear it. The only problem was we only had a back three. Smithy was on the halfway line waiting for the whistle. When it went, he sprinted forward and tackled Ardiles, the player given the task of knocking it long. Tackled? If it was done today, the offending player would be straight in front of the FA, with the possibility of civil action. Fortunately, the referee, like most of us, was ball watching so missed the tackle if not the Argentinian's scream! The next thing, Villa ran towards Smithy, shouting in broken English, 'Smith, you crazy man. *Loco!*'

With Ardiles writhing on the deck, Smithy turned to Villa and, pretending to carry a stretcher, replied, 'You next!' They may have been compatriots, but that stopped Villa in his tracks.

After the game had calmed down, Smithy incensed Spurs players further when he went up to Villa as we were defending a set piece and said, 'If you come any further, I will ram that World Cup up your arse!' On reflection, perhaps Wyndham was not that hard!

Smithy's actions almost caused a diplomatic rift between Argentina and the UK that predated the Falklands conflict by a few years. Keith Burkinshaw, the Spurs manager, accused Smithy of deliberately trying to injure a fellow professional, with Smithy replying that just because he was an expensive foreigner it did not mean he could not be tackled. Ardiles, unsurprisingly, didn't appear for the second half.

We went into a two-goal lead thanks to Robbie and Charlo, but despite heroics from Crudge and Speedy at the back we conceded two, a Glenn Hoddle penalty and an equaliser from Gerry Armstrong, who had played against us a few times in his Watford days. Having studied Spurs' performance at the Vetch from the dugout, Tosh decided to make a few changes for the second leg at White Hart Lane a week later. Even at this early stage of his managerial career, he was proving to be an astute tactician. He moved Speedy just in front of the back four and played himself as sweeper. His tactics were spot on, as, incredibly, we won 3–1, with me, Charlo and the manager getting the goals. Around 35,000 were in attendance. I think this was the game when the football world began to take an interest in what Tosh was achieving with this unfashionable club.

As well as Tosh's tactics being spot on, he also continued to develop his psychological approach. A few days before the game, he pinned up letters that had been sent to the club from London and Argentina. They all had a similar theme: if Smithy set foot on the pitch, he was going to stop a bullet. A little thing like that would not have stopped Smithy. The ex-Burnley and Wolves winger Steve Kindon was once asked how hard Tommy really was. Having faced him many times, he replied, 'All I can say is that Tommy was born on 5 April 1945 and a few weeks later Germany surrendered!' With only one substitute allowed in those days, there was a great chance they would get on when a team faced Smithy!

He might have won everything the game had to offer, but a few weeks later Smithy was to experience something for the first time in a long and illustrious career: the ignominy of being substituted. He had suffered a knock on the knee during a league game that was affecting his movement, so after an hour Tosh decided to make a change. Smithy politely questioned Tosh's judgement as he reluctantly left the field. A week later, Smithy had not recovered so missed out on the game against Blackpool, with Tosh asking him to keep an eye on things from the dugout. After an hour, Smithy decided to make a change. In those days, there were no fourth officials or electronic boards. The staff had to arrange the number of the player to be substituted on a board. Smithy walked to the side of the pitch and held up Tosh's number. 'What the fuck are you doing, Tommy? I'm the manager!' protested Tosh.

'No, son, I'm the manager today. You're off!' There were murders in the dressing-room after the game, but in the end Tosh did see the funny side. It was just lucky for Smithy that we won.

Even though we were top of the league by the end of September, we still appeared a little disjointed at times, conceding more goals than Tosh would have liked, the game against Rotherham at the

Vetch being a perfect example. Before the game, Wyndham had warned his central-defensive partner, Dave Bruton, how good their centre-forward, Dai Gwyther, was. We knew because Big Dai had played many times for the Swans before the club sold him to Halifax to raise much-needed cash. I regret never having had a chance to play alongside Dai, as I am sure we would have netted a few between us. Dave told Wyndham it would be no problem and that he should leave Dai to him. However, before we knew it, we were four down, with Big Dai getting three. The final score was 4–4, but Tosh was not happy with our sloppy defending in that and a few other games.

In October, Tosh decided that something had to be done. Out went Dave to Newport County for £15,000, to be replaced by the Aston Villa captain and Welsh international Leighton Phillips for £70,000. This was another example of the chairman trusting the manager's judgement and backing him without question.

As well as buying experienced players, Tosh was not afraid to put his faith in local lads, such as Mark Baker, a product of the Senior League who brazenly turned up at the Vetch and asked Tosh to give him a trial and ended up playing a few first-team games.

By New Year, we were three points behind Watford, and Tosh was again splashing the cash, bringing in Brian Attley for 20 grand from Cardiff. The utility player was Tosh's eighth signing. As we approached the end of February, our promotion hopes seemed to be fading, as we only took five points from eight games. Tosh had also applied to the Football Combination to raise the level of reserve-team football, although the club was not optimistic, as we had withdrawn twice before. The manager believed, with all due respect, that there was too much of a gap in standard between the part-time Welsh League and the first team. Having said that, Llanelli had twice beaten our reserves to the title in the preceding few years.

Unlike today, there was only one deadline for transfers, 29 March, so any player movement in or out had to be done by that date. We had won our first game in nine attempts during the first week of

March, so we wondered if there were going to be any more comings and goings. John Phillips, the Wales number-two, came in on loan from Chelsea as goalkeeping back-up for Crudge, as the only other keeper on the books was the sixteen-year-old Chris Sander.

Sunderland had rekindled their interest in me, and I did feel a little unsettled, as I was once again the subject of a lot of press interest. In early April, both Cally and I were selected for the Third Division team of the season by our fellow pros. Cally was a wonderful player and a model professional who inspired all those around him, especially the younger players. Bill Shankly likened him to a carrier pigeon: you gave him instructions and he delivered without error. Cally could pick a teammate out anywhere on the park with pinpoint accuracy. He and Smithy might have only travelled down from Liverpool on the day of the game or the day before, but in the little time he was at training he demonstrated good habits that the rest of us could learn from. Even the internationals amongst us were in awe of such a gentleman and wonderful pro. In fact, even though he was playing in the Third Division and coming to the end of an illustrious career, there were still some pundits calling on the England manager to consider him.

Towards the end of March, we beat arch rivals and fellow promotion candidates Watford 3–2 at the Vetch, and I scored with a diving header. It was the first time I had completed the 'perfect' hat-trick of left foot, right foot and header. The only thing was it had taken me three-quarters of a season to do it, as most players do it in the same game!

Such was our improved form that Tosh decided to come out of international retirement, although with such a small squad I hoped his decision would not backfire on us in the run-in, as Robbie, Leighton and I were already often away with Wales. More pressure was put on the squad when Phil Boersma broke his ankle at Swindon. With the crack being heard all around the ground, it was obvious that it was a career-threatening injury. Whether this affected our performance at home to Walsall in the next game, I'm not sure, but we soon found ourselves two down in a match we were expected to win. With 18,000 fans becoming frustrated and venting their disapproval, Tosh decided to put himself on in my place. Even though the boys pulled it back to 2–2, seemingly justifying the manager's decision, it did not prevent me being upset after the game, and I left the ground feeling dejected.

A few days later, I was back in the side to play Blackpool, and I had something to prove to the manager. We won 3–1, and I bagged one of the goals. Afterwards, Tosh took me to one side and told me that he had wanted to motivate me and was pleased that I had been disappointed to have been substituted and with the positive performance I had given in response. He said that he had used an experience of his own to motivate me. He told me that he had once been subbed in a UEFA Cup tie, storming out of the ground and listening to the result on his car radio on the way home. Tosh was certainly using the experience he had gained chasing all those honours to help us get out of the Third Division.

After losing 2–1 to Lincoln on 24 March, we put together a run of twelve games without defeat, which meant we were going into the last match of the season, against Chesterfield at home, one place behind Watford, who held the third promotion spot on goal difference. We had clawed our way back into the promotion hunt with our great end of season charge but still had to win this crucial final game. Chesterfield had beaten us in the away game, so it was never going to be a straightforward challenge, especially with so much at stake. We were soon one down, and both the players and crowd were becoming anxious until Alan Waddle equalised with a header.

The scene seemed set for a fairy-tale ending when Tosh came off the bench to replace Brian Attley. Soon afterwards, we won a free-kick in front of the North Bank. Danny Bartley floated the ball into the box, with Tosh leaping to meet it. It seemed as though time stood still as he hung in the air and arched his neck muscles. The next thing we knew, the ball was in the back of the net, and the whole place erupted.

It couldn't have been scripted any better. The player-manager had come off the bench to power home the winning header to secure us promotion. Not only had he won us the game, but the manner of his winning goal would have made his hero John Charles proud, and it helped us to move back to where we thought we belonged: the Second Division.

After our previous promotion, my thoughts were with Harry and how he had missed out on his dream. This time my thoughts turned to Wyndham, who had missed out on quite a few games because of the new signings. I was determined that we all share in our success, as Wyndham had been around when we had played in front of crowds around the 2,000 mark.

The day after the game, I was summoned to meet the manager and chairman, who informed me that they had refused an offer of £350,000 for me the previous morning. They did not say who the club was but told me that Leeds, Crystal Palace and Sunderland had made enquiries. Malcolm also said that we had made a profit over the last two seasons, so funds were available to strengthen the team. Tosh then outlined his plans: we were not going to consolidate in the Second but push on for the First. We were back in the second tier of the English game, with the youngest and most successful manager in the game. A new East Stand was being built, and a very lucrative contract was on the table waiting for my signature. Tosh told me to think things over on the club trip to Majorca, perhaps hoping that I could be won round.

I did give it some thought, but on a purely professional level I decided to go. On 14 May 1979, I thought I had ended my love affair with Swansea City. I signed for Leeds United for £400,000, making me the most expensive player outside of the top flight. The club had done everything to satisfy my ambition and desire. They put good money on the table, but I wanted to ply my trade at the very top straight away and not gamble on waiting another year.

In 1964, the Swans had sold Barrie Jones to Plymouth for a British record fee of £34,000. They had made ten times as much on me, so I suppose it was good business even if an angry Tosh did not think so at the time. A week later, the manager signed a new five-year deal, and there was money left over to buy Dave Rushbury, Tommy Craig and John Mahoney.

There were many important moments after I had signed for the Swans in 1972, but the most significant was when Harry turned me into a centre-forward. Before that, I had played one hundred and thirteen games and scored seven goals from midfield. Once Harry gave me more freedom, I played 135 league games, scoring 64 goals.

Even though he has never been renowned for his communication skills, a week later I received a letter from Tosh. In it he wrote, 'Watch what you eat and never forget you are Welsh.' He also said that half the fee would be waiting in his drawer to bring me back. I guess that was his way of wishing me good luck.

5

TO ELL AND BACK

On Tuesday, 15 May 1979, after more than seven happy years at the Swans, I became a Leeds United player, fulfilling my ambition of playing in the highest division at a club with a great tradition and name in the British game. There had been rumours that Liverpool were also interested in me, but I was happy to sign for Leeds, especially with their strong historical connections to Wales and Swansea in particular, and I would argue that two of the city's former sons, John Charles and Gary Sprake, would make an all-time greatest Leeds XI. When I moved to the Elland Road club in 1979, I was welcomed by my international colleagues Brian Flynn, Carl Harris and Byron Stevenson, as well as Swansea-born Gwyn Thomas, who played over 100 games for Leeds between 1975 and 1984. I had a young family at the time – my son Ian had been born six weeks earlier – so moving to a club with familiar faces from the Welsh international set-up was a real bonus and helped us to settle into a city that was quite a long way from our home in South Wales.

Although I had scored fifty-four league goals in two seasons for the Swans, I knew that the step up to the First Division would bring increasing demands on my game. I didn't feel too pressured, even though I knew that a lot would be expected of me, especially as my £400,000 transfer fee meant that I had become Leeds' most expensive ever signing, exceeding the £357,000 paid for Kevin Hird from Blackburn the previous season. I also replaced Leighton James as the most expensive Welsh player. Of course, it was only natural to be apprehensive about the impact and pressure that some of these records might have had, but I felt that my transfer was not nearly as high profile as some of the others taking place at that time. In February 1979, Brian Clough had paid the first £1-million fee for Trevor Francis, and shortly after my transfer to Leeds, Manchester City signed the uncapped Steve Daley from Wolves for £1,450,277. Naturally, the Leeds fans would be keen to make their own judgements about my performances.

One of the pieces of advice Tosh gave me was that at clubs like Leeds and Liverpool there would be far higher expectations of a player than there would be at the Swans. This proved to be very true, as in my first few weeks at Leeds I noticed that even in training there was a greater intensity and demand on players to perform.

If I did feel some pressure, it was surely nothing compared to that of the Leeds United and former Burnley manager Jimmy Adamson, who had spent over £1 million on new players in less than a year. As well as signing Kevin Hird and me, he had signed centre-back Paul Hart from Blackpool for £333,000 and striker John Hawley from Hull for £81,000. Although Adamson could point out to any detractors that a fifth-place finish the previous season had guaranteed the club a first season of European football since Leeds had been given a four-year ban after the 1975 European Cup final against Bayern Munich.

Despite the return of European competition for the forthcoming 1979–80 season, there still seemed to be an undercurrent of discontent at the club, as during the previous season average attendances had fallen to just under 27,000. The letter pages of the local papers were inundated that summer with fans complaining that £1.20 was far too much to pay to stand on the Elland Road terraces. It was no fault of Adamson, or indeed his predecessor Jimmy Armfield, as Don Revie's legacy was going to be difficult for any manager to live up to. After all, hadn't Brian Clough infamously managed only 44 days as Leeds manager? Revie's record between 1965 and 1975 was the equal of any manager in Britain, his team winning two league titles, two European trophies, and the FA and League Cups, not to mention coming runners-up in the league a further five times. I think that Revie's legacy obviously did hang heavily over the club in those first few years after he left, and the manager, players and fans all felt it to varying extents. However, Adamson convinced me that he was going to bring back the glory days to the club, and, of course, I wanted to help him to achieve his aims for Leeds.

However, the transfer nearly didn't go ahead at all, as I was made a much better offer by another club at the last moment. On the morning I was travelling to Leeds to sign the paperwork and undertake my medical, I called into the Vetch to say some goodbyes. As I was about to leave, one of the office staff shouted to me that there was a call from someone who wouldn't say who they were, only that it was important. When I picked up the phone, I was surprised when the caller introduced himself as Alan Harris, the number two to Terry Venables at Crystal Palace, who had just won promotion to the top flight as Second Division champions. He asked me if I had signed for Leeds, and when I replied that I hadn't yet but was on my way to Yorkshire, he offered me a larger weekly wage than I was going to be on at Leeds. I never had an agent during my playing career, but if I had, given such a scenario, I could probably have doubled my weekly wage.

The offer was obviously tempting, as the money was very good and Terry Venables was known to be an excellent coach, who some commentators argued was building the team of the '80s at Palace, and I was obviously flattered, but I never really considered it seriously, as I had shaken on the deal with Leeds. I am quite old fashioned and had given my word, even if it did mean that I was going to lose out on a substantial sum of money.

In July 1979, a pre-season tour of Germany marked my debut for Leeds, and I scored in a 3–2 win over FC Schalke. During the tour, some worrying rumours were circulating in the press back home about the future of Leeds captain Tony Currie. It was alleged that Currie's wife was unhappy in Leeds and wanted to move back to London, where they were both originally from. The issue of the midfielder's future at the club seemed to dominate the rest of the pre-season and was certainly unsettling for the fans, who worshipped him. Eventually, the club reluctantly put their captain up for sale for £600,000, and by early August the situation had become so tense between the player and management that an offer of only £400,000 was accepted from QPR. Leeds' loss was obviously the Loftus Road club's gain, as Currie was one of the most skilful players of his generation, the type who could score or create a goal with one moment of magic. I was very disappointed, as one of the reasons I signed for the club was to play in the same side as quality players such as Tony.

Over that summer, full-back Frank Gray also left the club in a £500,000 deal that took him to Notts Forest to replace Frank Clark, who was retiring from playing. Frank Gray was a classy full-back who had been at Elland Road for nine years and had played in the losing 1975 European Cup-final team. Again, I felt it was a huge blow to lose such a quality player from the squad, although it worked out well for Frank himself, as he won a European Cup-winner's medal in his first season under Brian Clough as Forest astounded their critics by retaining the trophy. Although I didn't know most of my new colleagues very well, I did get the sense that the rest of the squad also felt that selling these key players was a huge blow to the team's chances of challenging at the top of the league.

At least there was a silver lining to Frank Gray's departure for my Welsh international colleague Byron Stevenson, whose future at the club now seemed more secure. Byron was a quality defender who had initially been signed as a replacement when Norman Hunter retired but had suffered to some extent at Leeds by the perception of him as a utility player and had up to that time never really had the chance to secure a settled role in the team. I think that despite the 'utility tag', Byron realised that to play regularly at a top team like Leeds he had to be prepared to be flexible.

I knew Byron well from the Wales squad, and he really went out of his way to help me and the family settle in Leeds. He was a passionate Welshman and very proud of his 15 caps for his country, and he was one of the most enthusiastic when we joined with our fellow Celts to play against England in training. When our careers with Wales finished, we did lose touch a bit, as Byron stayed in Leeds to run a pub before returning home to Llanelli. After he came home, we did meet up, playing in quite a few charity games and catching up on old times. Although I was aware that Byron was ill, it was a huge shock to hear the news in September 2007 that he had died of cancer at the tragically young age of 50. He was a lovely guy and a model professional, and he will be fondly remembered by everybody who knew him.

If the sale of Currie and Gray in the summer of 1979 sent ominous shockwaves through the city with regards to the team's prospects for the forthcoming season, the decision to return the old peacock badge to the Leeds shirt should perhaps have given all associated with the club even more to be concerned about. Don Revie was notoriously superstitious, and one of his first actions as Leeds manager in the early 1960s was to remove the peacock emblem from the team's shirts, as he believed that birds were inherently unlucky. Judging by how the season turned out for both the club and me personally, perhaps more attention should have been paid by the management to the intuition of the man in the famous old blue suit. At first, my career with Leeds seemed to blossom, but over time lady luck seemed to turn against me, apparently reinforcing Revie's warnings about the misfortune associated with the controversial emblem.

I made my league debut for Leeds away at Bristol City on the first Saturday of the 1979–80 season, and I couldn't have asked for a much better first appearance for my new club. Partnering Ray Hankin up front, I scored both our goals in a 2–2 draw. This was especially pleasing, as I was being watched by a load of family and friends who had made the short journey across the Severn Bridge from Wales. I put us in the lead after only nine minutes, but, to be honest, we were mostly second best for the remainder of the match. The inexperienced defence who hadn't really played together struggled, and although Brian Flynn worked tirelessly in midfield the absence of Currie was immediately felt, as we missed his quality and ability to create space in the middle of the park. City deservedly equalised with a 33rd-minute penalty and went a goal up from a free-kick after 65 minutes. However, with less than ten minutes left, Hankin got his head to a deep cross, the flick-on landed at my feet and I was more than happy to sweep the ball home for the equaliser.

I was obviously really pleased with my debut, but after the game Ray Hankin seemed less happy and put in a transfer request that remained in place until he finally quit the club for Canadian team Vancouver Whitecaps the following March.

Over the first two months of the season, our performances could be described as steady rather than spectacular, as we only lost one of our first seven games. Despite our defence tightening up, we were still struggling to create chances, and after beating Everton 2–0 in our first home game we only scored five goals in the next six league games. The lack of creative flair in midfield meant that we suffered up front from a lack of clear-cut scoring chances, so it was a little bit of a surprise when Adamson bought two defensive midfielders: Brian Greenhoff from Manchester United for £350,000 and Gary Hamson from Sheffield United for £140,000. Both Brian and Gary were dedicated pros, but they were probably not the sort of signings that the Leeds fans were expecting to replace terrace favourite Tony Currie. In defence of Adamson, there probably wasn't a quality midfielder with flair available at that time, especially at the price Leeds were able to pay. Brian's brother Jimmy had actually started his career at Elland Road under Don Revie before going on to have an even more successful career, firstly with Stoke City and then with Manchester United, where both Jimmy and Brian played together for a short period.

During September, we had notable draws at home against Arsenal and away to reigning European Champions Notts Forest without really performing to our best. However, the highlight for me was the game at Elland Road against Liverpool on Saturday, 15 September. At that time, the Anfield club were probably the best team in Europe, and despite losing their European crown to Forest the previous year had dominated domestic and Continental football over a five-year period. Although comparisons between teams from different eras are often contentious, I think there are very few football commentators or fans who would disagree that this particular Liverpool team were up there with the greatest of all time. In front of 39,779 fans, the biggest league crowd of my career thus far, the Liverpool starting XI contained seven England internationals, plus quality Scottish stars Kenny Dalglish and Alan Hansen, and Avi Cohen, their new Israeli signing who was making his debut.

In a typically close-fought clash between the two clubs, we again struggled to create clear-cut chances, despite constant pressure, and Dalglish poached a goal with only ten minutes left. In the final minute, we launched one final attack towards the mass ranks of the home fans at the Gelderd End, otherwise known as the Kop. As the ball was pumped into the Reds' penalty area, a half-cleared defensive header landed at my feet at the edge of the box. I instinctively hit it on the half-volley, and as it went flying by Ray Clemence the roar from the home fans on the Kop gave me a real adrenalin rush. The feeling of pride and satisfaction is difficult to describe fully.

Despite the team scrapping for results, including a series of hard-fought draws, we knew that we weren't really gelling as a unit, and there was an undercurrent of pressure affecting the squad. Given our general lack of goals, the sale of John Hawley in late September to

Sunderland for £100,000 seemed another strange decision by the manager. John had only signed for the club the previous season and was a popular and hard-working striker who had netted 16 league goals for the club during the 1978–79 campaign. His replacement, Wayne Entwistle, made the opposite journey from Roker Park for £80,000 but never really made an impact at Elland Road, only playing ten times for the first team before being released on a free transfer to Blackpool the following season.

Any hopes of matching the previous season's run in the League Cup, when the team had reached the semi-finals, were dented in the first round when we lost to Arsenal. After a 1–1 draw at home, we still felt we were in the tie when we travelled to Highbury. However, in what I regard as one of the worst team performances I ever played in, we lost 7–0 and crashed out 8–1 on aggregate. I felt sorry for David Harvey, who could only look on as the goals flew in past him, unable to do anything about any of them. At the end of the game, Dave seemed shell-shocked, and it was only later that we found out that over a decade earlier as a young pro he had been on the end of another 7–0 League Cup defeat in London against West Ham – it must have been a real sense of déjà vu for the Scottish keeper. Dave was a great keeper and a really nice guy who had been at the club since 1965, so I felt for him when he was replaced by John Lukic as the Leeds number one. A few weeks later, he left for Vancouver, but Dave's ties with Leeds were strong, and he returned to the club in 1982, playing with distinction for a further three seasons under Eddie Gray's management.

After the League Cup debacle, we were at least offered some immediate redemption in a cup competition when the first-round draw of the UEFA Cup saw us paired against Valetta of Malta. I vividly remember the away leg in Malta, more for off-the-field events than the match itself, which we won 4–0 thanks to an Arthur Graham hat-trick. I had played in Valetta with Wales two months previously, so I knew it would be very hot and that the pitch was dreadful and the facilities at the ground were shocking. As we arrived off the plane, we were greeted by hundreds of well-wishers, who turned out to be the local branch of the Leeds United Supporters Club.

Before the game, as anybody who has been to Malta will verify, the local people couldn't have been more friendly and accommodating, so it was a little bit of a shock when we arrived at the ground to be met by a record crowd of 18,000 hemmed in behind wire fences, baying for our blood as firecrackers and flares flew from the terraces. The other thing I remember about the match was that the Leeds coaching staff had decided that we would get changed in the hotel before the game and go straight back there on the coach to shower afterwards because the facilities on offer at the ground were so poor. In the home leg, we again won comfortably, and a 3–0 victory would have been more like a cricket score if it wasn't for the heroics of their keeper Frank Grima, who made a number of brilliant saves, including stopping a Kevin Hird penalty. I had put us ahead with the first move of the game, timed at 20 seconds, which was (and I think probably still is) the fastest goal scored by Leeds in European competition.

In the league that October, our results continued to be indifferent: we beat Ipswich and Southampton, drew with Brighton but lost 2–1 at home to Spurs. I particularly remember the Southampton game at the Dell when I scored one of my best-ever goals as the team recorded their first league victory away from home for seven months. With ten minutes of the game to go, we were drawing 1–1, and I received a pass from Jeff Chandler about 20 yards inside our own half. I don't know why, but instead of playing a simple pass out to the wing I ran inside, and about fifty yards later, after beating three or four Saints players, I found myself at the edge of their box. I decided to have a crack with my left foot and was delighted when a 20-yard curler went in past their keeper Terry Gennoe. I was really proud of the strike, especially as it won goal of the month on *Match of the Day*, which was always a great accolade.

As the clocks were turned back to mark the beginning of winter, our performances continued to be below par, losing three consecutive league games. All three displays were very poor. After losing 3–0 at Coventry, we then went down 5–1 to Everton at Goodison. But by far the most disappointing defeat was a 3–1 home reverse against foot-of-the-table Bristol City, which meant we were in the bottom four. This led to a small section of the Elland Road crowd demanding the resignation of Jimmy Adamson.

As a team, confidence was low, and in those situations luck always seems to desert you, as was the case for Brian Flynn, who seriously damaged his ankle ligaments in the Coventry game, leading to him being out of first-team action for four months. Brian had been one of the few players in the team who had been playing consistently well and one of the few positives in a struggling midfield. Having joined Leeds for £175,000 from Burnley in 1977, he'd immediately forged a very effective midfield partnership with Tony Currie, and his voracious appetite for hard work and clever passing made him a firm favourite with the Leeds fans.

If there was pressure on the team and the management, this only intensified as we crashed out 4–0 on aggregate in the second round of the UEFA Cup to Universitatea Craiova of Romania. This was especially disappointing for the club, as they had been keen to put behind them the negative memories of the European Cup final at the Parc des Princes four years earlier. The result of the final against Bayern Munich in May 1975 was seen as a travesty of justice by Leeds fans – and most neutrals, come to that.

Leeds fans had been used to success in European competition and the team's record was second to none, having appeared in five major finals in eight years between 1967 and 1975. However, only 14,000 fans turned up on 7 November 1979 to see us lose 2–0 to the Romanians at Elland Road, which seemed to be an indication of a large section of the fans' disillusionment with the team's league performances. The fact that the Romanians, like most Eastern European teams at that time, were a well-organised and technically excellent side was no consolation to the Leeds faithful, who again saw the glory days of the Revie era drifting further and further over the horizon. It was after the home leg that Leeds chairman Manny Cussins gave manager Adamson the customary 'vote of confidence'. It later emerged after Adamson had left Leeds that the board were only prepared to give him up until the New Year to see if results improved.

What the team needed to break the despondency that was circling over the club was a stroke of good luck or an inspirational performance. It came in the unlikely form of 17-year-old trainee Terry Connor, a local lad who still watched the majority of home games from the terraces. His winning goal in a 1–0 defeat of West Brom seemed to immediately act as a spark for the home fans. Supporters appreciate home-grown players, especially ones brought up as fans of the club they go on to play for.

The defeat of the Baggies was definitely the catalyst the team, and particularly the under pressure Leeds manager, needed, and we went on a run that saw us only lose one of the next ten games, winning six and drawing three. One notable performance from the team was when we secured a 1–1 draw against Man United thanks to a late Terry Connor equaliser. A good result against the Reds always went down particularly well with the Leeds fans, especially at Old Trafford. Terry was bringing the real enthusiasm of youth to the team and showed no signs of nerves, despite his inexperience. He was hugely popular with the home fans, and there was a lot of discontent when he was controversially transferred to Brighton in March 1983 in a swap deal for Andy Ritchie.

By the time we lost for the first time in ten games, 3–1 away at Middlesbrough on Boxing Day, only two players had played in all twenty-two league games: me and club captain Trevor Cherry. I was obviously pleased to have been ever present but still slightly disappointed with my return of only four league goals, and I am sure that some Leeds fans had doubts about my contribution to the team's form. I felt that the fact that only two players played in every match up to that point showed the transition the team was undergoing and to some extent seemed to reflect Adamson's indecision in finding his best side. In fact, Terry Connor was the fifth striking partner that I had played with, and the season was only halfway through.

One of the team's main problems was that we weren't scoring enough, which was reinforced by the fact that my four goals still made me joint top scorer with Terry and penalty-taker Kevin Hird. I did feel that my partnership with Terry was beginning to work well, and despite not scoring regularly I was happy with my general contribution, as we had gone on a run that had taken us from the relegation places to the top ten in the division.

I have to admit that it did take me a while to adjust to the higher standards required in the First Division, and even keeping up to the high standard of training sessions was initially difficult, but by Christmas I felt that I was settling into life in the top league. However, I was carrying a slight groin strain after the Middlesbrough defeat, so I was advised to rest, missing my first games of the season: the 2–2 draw against Norwich at Carrow Road and the home victory over Derby on New Year's Day. Jimmy Adamson told me that even though the goals were not flowing for me yet, he was very happy with my overall contribution to the team's improved performances, and as soon as I'd had a week off I would be back in the side, as he hoped we would push on towards competing for a European place.

I returned to the squad for the third-round FA Cup tie at home to Notts Forest. During the week leading up to the game, the country was in the grip of a big freeze, but Leeds had undersoil heating, so the match was definitely going to go ahead. On the Thursday before the tie, Adamson pulled me aside in training and asked me how I was feeling. I replied that I felt fine. He said, 'Excellent, Curt, but I think given the weather we won't risk it on Saturday. But you'll definitely be back in the team for the trip to Highbury.'

My parents had been spending some time with us over the holidays in Yorkshire, as my injury had given me my first New Year off in nearly a decade. Given that I wasn't going to play against Forest, my parents decided to extend their holiday by a few days. On the Saturday morning, the phone went early, and I received the message that there had been a few last-minute injuries and I should report to Elland Road as soon as possible. When I arrived, I was met by Jimmy Adamson, who said he was sorry but he was going to need me to play after all, up front with Terry Connor. I think my dad was quite pleased about it, as he always liked to watch me play, but my mum was less keen and felt it was far too cold to spend the afternoon at a freezing Elland Road. I'm glad she wasn't there, as Saturday, 5 January 1980 is a day I'll never forget, one that I thought marked a premature end to my football career.

The game started badly for us when old boy Frank Gray scored with a really well-taken free-kick, which had been awarded after Forest's very first attack. The afternoon was bitterly cold, but we were still in the match when shortly before half-time Eddie Gray played a ball over the top of their defence. As I chased it down, Peter Shilton came out to try and cut out the pass. It was a classic 50–50 situation, and neither of us pulled out of the challenge. Peter went for the ball fair and square and just managed to parry it away from me as we both collided.

I knew it was bad straight away. I had a shooting pain that went all the way up my right leg. As I was stretchered off behind the goal, I was in so much pain that I almost passed out, but I still heard a faint roar, which I later found out followed Garry Birtles putting them 2–0 up at the other end of the pitch. Although the local press reported that I had strained my ligaments and would be out for a few weeks, I knew it was far more serious than that. What I didn't know was just how serious the injury actually was.

As well as rupturing my knee ligaments, I had torn part of my hamstring so badly that it had actually come off the bone. My operation took place in the famous St James Hospital, which was known in Leeds as Jimmy's. I was very worried and in the first few weeks after the injury seriously feared my football career might be finished. When I met with the specialist, he told me it was a case of good news and bad news. The good news was that I wouldn't walk with a limp for the rest of my life. I interrupted him there and then and said, 'OK, don't even give me the bad news.'

The first plaster, which I had to wear for the first few weeks, was at least two foot six inches long and extended from my ankle to the top of my thigh. It drove me mad, and even the most routine daily tasks became very difficult. When this was removed, the replacement plaster was only slightly shorter, and I had to wear it for a further three months. These were probably the most uncomfortable and frustrating few months of my life. By the time the second plaster was taken off at Easter, my right leg was virtually half the size of my other one due to muscle wastage.

In early April, I began my rehabilitation programme, which was extremely tedious and often very lonely. As any ex-professional footballer who has suffered a serious injury would tell you, the recovery time spent in the treatment room and the fitness centre is very boring, and the tedium is often tinged with a feeling of isolation. Being away from the banter of the dressing-room, you feel you are not really part of the squad and that events are unfolding without you. Geoff Ladley, the Leeds physiotherapist, was brilliant, and his constant support and encouragement made a difficult time far more bearable. He was always positive, telling me that pre-season in July was my target and that if I worked hard and remained positive, he knew I could make it.

At first, I had to take my rehab in small steps, with some light walking followed by a programme of swimming and cycling before being allowed to undertake some easy running by the end of May. At each stage of my rehabilitation, Geoff was there with his measuring tape to test how much the leg muscle had developed and to make a positive comment on the progress I was making. By June, I was able to jog with little or no pain, and thanks to Geoff's help I was ready to rejoin the rest of the squad for pre-season training. Although I am generally a very positive person, I know that without Geoff's constant enthusiasm and hard work I would have found the struggle to get fit far more daunting, and I can't thank him enough for all his hard work.

As I undertook my recovery programme, the team eventually finished 11th in the league, winning 40 points from 42 league games. Despite missing the last twenty games of the season, I was still third-top scorer behind Kevin Hird with eight and Terry Connor with five. It was clear that the team had suffered from a goal-scoring drought, which many critics directly related to the sale of Tony Currie to QPR the previous summer. It was evident that Adamson was going to be under immense pressure to improve results at the beginning of the 1980–81 season and that the team needed more goals. These factors had prompted the Leeds manager to try to bolster his goal-scoring options by signing the Argentinian Alex Sabella from Sheffield United for £400,000 and Rangers centre-forward Derek Parlane for £160,000.

Me and my new colleagues undertook a pre-season tour to Germany and Switzerland. If I was concerned about whether I was fully recovered, my doubts were answered in the game against Grasshoppers of Zurich. In probably the most unpleasant friendly I ever played in, the Swiss defenders decided to use me as target practice every time I got the ball. Any worries about an injury hangover were soon forgotten, as my immediate concern was just to survive the 90 minutes.

Even though I had successfully got through pre-season – Swiss defenders aside – I knew the real test of my recovery would begin when the league started in earnest. I was selected to start in our first two league games, against Aston Villa and Middlesbrough, but we lost both games, and, in all honesty, I was well off the pace. Despite a good pre-season, the fact that I hadn't played a competitive match since early January had clearly affected my performances, and I didn't really play well in either game. I was obviously disappointed but not surprised when Adamson told me that he was going to put me in the reserves for a few weeks to try to build up my match sharpness and fitness.

In fairness, the move worked, and although I missed being part of the first team I played in four reserve games in a fortnight and scored in every match. The word from reserve-team coach Dave Merrington was that Adamson had told him that he felt I was ready to return to first-team action and that I would be in the side for the game against Spurs the following Saturday at Elland Road. A factor probably in my favour was that the first team had only won one of their first six games, and even at that early stage was worryingly in the relegation places.

Unfortunately, as is often the way in football, events overtook these plans, and on Monday, 8 September, following a 3–0 reverse at Stoke, the Leeds board sacked Jimmy Adamson. Adamson's period as Leeds manager was probably seen by many as fairly unsuccessful, especially in comparison to his 30-year association with Burnley as both a player and manager. However, I think that whoever took over in the immediate years after Don Revie was always going to struggle, just as Jimmy Armfield found when he was manager in the mid-1970s. I had a lot of time for Jimmy Adamson, always finding him to be very fair and a manager who talked a lot of sense about the game, never blowing a fuse unless he was really pushed. In terms of coaching, he didn't really run day-to-day training, but when he did run sessions they were highly enjoyable. I think Jimmy was a highly capable manager, but perhaps the task of rebuilding Leeds was a challenge too far for him.

Later that week, it was announced that the new manager would be Barnsley manager and former Leeds favourite Allan Clarke. England international Clarke had joined Leeds from Leicester in 1969 and proved himself along with Jimmy Greaves and Denis Law to be one of the great goal poachers of his generation. Clarke was an instant hit with the Leeds fans and scored 151 goals for the club in 366 games. However, although his playing record was never in doubt, his managerial credentials had yet to be really tested.

Clarke had a very serious management style and although not a Yorkshireman by birth had quickly developed the dour personality often associated with sportsmen from that county. At the beginning of his first training session, he sat the squad down and laid out his plans for the club's future success. We would win the league title that season, immediately followed the next season by triumph in the European Cup. Given the fact that the club was in the bottom three after two months of the season, I think everybody was a little stunned to say the least. I was actually sitting between two of Clarke's former colleagues and Revie legends Eddie Gray and Paul Madeley, and I'm sure I could hear sniggering from either side of me as Clarke set out his somewhat ambitious targets.

Although Revie's team had gained a reputation for being over-competitive, which over the years gave rise to the 'Dirty Leeds' tag, I don't think you would find two more classy players and real gentlemen in the game than Eddie and Paul. Paul was a real team man who played in every outfield position for Leeds in his 536 appearances in 17 years at Elland Road. Eddie was a world-class player, and even though when I was at Leeds he was in the twilight of his career he always had time on the ball, which was the mark of a quality player. I also have to say that Eddie is probably one of the nicest guys I've ever come across in professional football.

I wasn't selected for the first XI by Clarke in his early weeks at the club, but after a 4–1 defeat at Sunderland in late September he picked me in the team that achieved a 1–1 draw away at Ipswich. I kept my place in the next two games, beating Everton and Manchester City, but was dropped again after a 2–1 loss to Wolves at Molineux. Although I obviously didn't realise it at the time, the game against

Wolves proved to be my final act in a Leeds shirt. At least both the Elland Road faithful and I had some positive memories of my last home game for the club, as I scored the winner in the scrappy 1–0 win over Everton.

Despite being a goal poacher himself, Clarke had set out his stall as a more defensive manager and increasingly selected only one striker in home matches as well as those away from Elland Road. For large sections of some games, we barely crossed the halfway line, and I had an increasing feeling that Clarke felt I wasn't suitable for the style of football his teams were going to play. After the Everton game, their skipper Mick Lyons was quoted in the press as saying that Leeds were the most negative home side he had ever had the displeasure of playing against.

By early December, I had played in only six first-team games that season, and when Swansea tabled an offer of £175,000, less than half they had sold me for, I was more than happy to return to South Wales. I also think that Clarke was more than happy to let me go. Maybe he saw me as a flair player and getting rid of me was a chance to put his own stamp on the team. Leeds ended up ninth in the league that season but only scored 39 league goals, and their top scorer was my Wales colleague Carl Harris, who was an excellent player but a winger rather than an out-and-out striker.

During the following 1981–82 season, I was famously to play against Leeds in the First Division, but while the Swans initially prospered, finishing sixth, my former club was sadly relegated. Clarke faced the inevitable sack and was soon joined by former teammates Eddie Gray and Billy Bremner, both of whom failed to return the club to the top flight. I think that the Leeds board should share responsibility for the club's decline in the 1980s, as they were reluctant to allow other managers to spend any money after giving some transfer money to Jimmy Adamson. I think the club's decline from greatness was only worsened in the eyes of the fans by the sustained success of Liverpool, who appointed their managers and coaches in-house and thus continued to dominate domestic and European football.

I was sorry to be leaving Leeds, who were and are a big club, but I was delighted to be returning to Swansea. I had no bitter feelings about my time in Yorkshire and just felt that things hadn't worked out for me. I certainly wasn't looking for anybody to blame for my relatively disappointing 18 months with the club. I think if it wasn't for the serious injury and the fact that this kept me out of football for eight months, I would have remained in the first team and seen out my three-year contract. Allan Clarke never actually told me that I had no future at Leeds, but I just got the feeling that my prospects weren't good and that leaving was probably the best thing for me and the club.

There are a lot of Leeds fans living in South Wales, and I often get asked about my time at Elland Road and why things didn't really work out for me. As I've said, I think one of the major problems at that time for any manager, not just Jimmy Adamson or Allan Clarke, was the long shadow that Don Revie's legacy had left upon the club. I also think that mistakes were made, especially in selling popular players who had done well for the team, such as Tony Currie, Frank Gray and John Hawley.

If I was given the option again of going back to May 1979, I would still make the same decision and sign for Leeds. Although I haven't actually returned to Elland Road in the last 25 years, I still look out for their results and have been disappointed with their decline in recent years. I was particularly hoping that they would beat Doncaster in the play-off final in 2008 and join the Swans in the Championship. I'm sure, however, that with huge crowds averaging over 25,000 Leeds will soon rise back up the league, and I look forward to the day when the Swans will face them again, hopefully in a Premier League fixture.

6

TOP FLIGHT

Some dates are etched in my mind, and 12 December 1980 is no exception. When I was told to go to the manager's office, I did get the feeling that somebody was interested in signing me, but I was shocked to hear that the club given permission to talk to me were the Swans. I had kept an eye on their results, and they were on an eight-match unbeaten run that had taken them to fourth in the league. Despite the good form, the team were far from free scoring, and results were being ground out.

I met Tosh, and he said that the fee to take me home was a reasonable one. I signed on the Friday and watched the lads the following day against Newcastle. There were rumours circulating that Tosh was going to sell David Giles to finance my move. Whether it was true or another of his ploys to get the best out of his players is difficult to say. It seemed to work, though, as the lads produced, so I was told, their best performance of the season, beating Newcastle 4–0.

The following Monday, Tosh produced another shock with another big-name international signing, the Wales rugby union scrum-half Gareth Edwards on a part-time contract. Gareth had been on the Swansea staff as a schoolboy before gaining a scholarship at Millfield

School and went on to win 53 consecutive rugby caps for his country. He never played a first-team game for the Swans, though, so I guess it was just a publicity stunt.

I did not have to wait long for my first game, coming on as a sub against what were by now our perennial rivals, Watford. Not long after going on, we were awarded a penalty after Robbie was tripped. Teams usually nominate a penalty-taker before the game, and perhaps we had, but when it came to taking it everyone turned their back, so I stepped up and thankfully converted it in front of 13,000 fans, our second-highest gate of the season. We had climbed to third in the table behind West Ham and Chelsea after a Boxing Day defeat of Bristol Rovers, which was our highest league position for 25 years. The next day, we were up against arch-rivals Cardiff City. These days, both fixtures would probably be deemed 'bubble games' and would have been played weeks if not months apart. (Bubble games are ones in which fans are only allowed to travel with the official club coaches, on which the tickets are issued, in order to prevent independent travel.) Then we just had to get on with it, and I guess playing two derby games in as many days caught up with us, as we threw away a two-goal lead in the last ten minutes, drawing 3–3.

Off the pitch, the directors were looking for ways of raising money to help strengthen our drive for promotion. One idea they came up with was the £100 'Building Bonds' scheme, whereby fans could guarantee their seats for ten years and then get their money back. Back then, I do not suppose that ten years was considered a very long time in the topsy-turvy world of Swansea City!

As we entered the New Year, we believed that we were serious candidates for promotion. We were on an unbeaten run of eight games in the league and next up were the FA Cup holders West Ham in what was billed as the 'Game of the Season' in some quarters. Even though I got our goal, we conceded three and doubts were creeping in, as we had lost 5–0 at home to Middlesbrough in the FA Cup the previous week. The following week, the old merry-go-round was in operation again, as Cally announced he was leaving after two and a half years. A week or so before, Alan Waddle had also departed, joining Newport County for £80,000. Cally was the consummate professional and in his 76 games for us had brought the right habits and helped greatly with the development of the younger players.

Tosh decided to send us off to Spain, because we didn't have a game the following week as a result of our cup exit. It was meant to be a bonding session, but when we got back a rift developed between the manager and one of the club's most experienced players, Leighton Phillips. After losing the next game 2–1 to QPR, Tosh decided to do away with the sweeper system and put the blame for our sticky patch on Leighton, who had played with Tosh at Cardiff and was his international teammate. Leighton was dropped to the Welsh League and told to train on his own away from the first team. Tosh also made it clear to Leighton that if he was not happy with his decision, he could leave, and there were also rumours that the defender had been suspended. This was purely conjecture, however, because whenever Tosh disciplined a player, it remained between the two of them. One thing is for sure, though: there was nothing like a spell in the Welsh League to bring a senior player down to earth! One week Leighton was turning out at Maesteg Park, the following week he was captaining his country against the Republic of Ireland.

I guess this was another example of how ruthless managers can be. In this case, Tosh was not going to allow sentiment to cloud his judgement, although I am glad that he and Leighton are still friends today. Nobody else had to endure what Leighton went through, because Tosh pulled out of the Welsh League that year, arguing that it was doing nothing for the development of the kids at the club.

The following week, Tosh signed the Bosnian Ante Rajković for £100,000 to join fellow countryman Jimmy Hadžiabdić, and both went on to obtain legendary status with the Vetch Field faithful. In less than six months, Tosh had spent around £455,000 whilst only bringing in the £80,000 for Willy Waddle. Ante made his debut in a

7–1 friendly win against Red Star Belgrade. They were great signings, because not only were they both terrific players, they could help each other come to terms with the language and culture, although we as players also did our best to help with their linguistic skills, and after a few months both could order steak and effing chips! Culturally, they took a little longer to adapt. For example, Jimmy used to park his car outside the Vetch but did not know that he was getting tickets for parking illegally. He thought fans were leaving him notes to autograph. It was only when the local council informed the police that the club became aware of it.

When the civil war broke out in the former Yugoslavia, I remember Leighton James asking Jimmy if he would consider returning home to join the war effort. 'Yes, when it reaches my village!' Jimmy replied.

'Whereabouts is that?' enquired Leighton.

'Birchgrove!'

The end of February saw us get our next win, against Derby County, with Leighton James firing home a hat-trick, including one of his specials from 25 yards. Leighton was a truly world-class player, and I am still undecided if he was right or left footed. He had wonderful balance, could pass and shoot with either foot, and would have graced any team of that era, or indeed any era.

By the end of March, following a defeat at Grimsby, we had slipped out of the title race, and we really needed to put together an unbeaten run until the end of the season if we were going to gain promotion to the First Division. We started April with a 1–0 win against Derby, courtesy of a Charlo goal. April also saw us win a two-legged Welsh Cup semi against Wrexham, with Dai Davies in goal, which guaranteed us European football once more, as we were up against Hereford in the final. (Playing an English opponent in the final meant automatic qualification for Europe because English teams were not allowed to represent Wales in Continental competition.) In the league, a 2–1 victory over Bristol Rovers meant that the last promotion spot was going to be a three-horse race between Blackburn, Luton and us.

Next up were Chelsea, who two days before the game parted company with their manager Geoff Hurst, replacing him with his assistant Bobby Gould. This was the game that made us realise we really could achieve our promotion dream, as the whole team gelled and everyone played well. Jimmy got a goal in a 3–0 win, with the scoreline flattering Chelsea. When people talk about attacking full-backs, Jimmy was up there with the best.

In our penultimate game, we drew 2–2 with Luton, which meant we had to beat Preston to go up; a draw would not be enough. When I started my career, this is what I always dreamed about: making it to the very top with the Swans. It was only going to take 90 minutes to decide our fate, but the days leading up to the game seemed like an eternity.

The good thing was that we knew exactly what we had to do before the Preston game: win the game and we would be promoted to the top tier of English football for the first time in the club's history. The situation was entirely in our own hands, and the pressure on us to win was enormous.

There was unprecedented coverage from the media, with both national and local television, radio and newspapers camped around the club. Then, of course, there were the supporters, especially the older ones, who wanted us to settle an old score: the FA Cup semi-final defeat of 1964 against the same team.

It was almost a relief when we set off on the Friday before the game to make the long journey north. For our part, we just wanted to win the match so that we would be playing in the top flight the following year. We were very conscious, nevertheless, of not letting down our supporters, family, friends and each other.

Over the season, we had acquired such a strong mentality that we were determined nothing was going to stop us. We really were a tight set of lads. I remember on one occasion we went out midweek to wet David Giles' baby's head. We stayed out until the early hours of the morning, going around the town on a pub crawl. While in our last port of call, The Bay View, just down Oystermouth Road and run by ex-Swan Peter Davies, the police raided the premises and booked all the players. The majority of the officers were Swans supporters, and while they took down our particulars we signed autographs for their friends and families. When we reported for training a few hours later, we were summoned to a meeting by Tosh. He demanded to know how many of us were out and was taken aback by Leighton's reply. 'Twenty-three, Boss!' Tosh was angrier with the couple of lads who didn't make it and gave them a bollocking about lack of team bonding and the need to stick together.

Bill Shankly came to our hotel on the Friday evening, and Tosh asked him to address the players. In typical style, he gave a rousing speech about grabbing the opportunity and seizing the day. He seemed to sense our mood about the fans when he told us that 10,000 were coming up to support us and we were not to let them down. We probably did not need the reminder, but it just gave us that extra sense of responsibility and spurred us on even more.

The Preston game was not the first that Shanks attended. He was a regular visitor to our hotel and dressing-room whenever we played up north. His appearance was very ordinary, just like a favourite uncle, but when he spoke he lit up the room. He spoke so passionately and with so much enthusiasm that you could not help but be inspired by him. After one game, he came up to me and told me how well I had played and what a great player I was. When someone like Bill Shankly speaks to you like that, you feel ten feet tall, and I will always treasure that moment. Much fuss was made about Tosh wearing a Liverpool shirt during the minute's silence when the Swans played Liverpool at Anfield after Shanks' passing. I thought it was a great and fitting tribute to an absolute icon who had been a major influence on Tosh's career.

The rest of the Friday evening and the next morning were pretty normal, as we followed the same routines and pre-match preparation as though it was any other game. It was travelling to the match from the hotel, however, when all the nerves really kicked in, for all we could see on the journey to Deepdale were Swans scarves and flags. I think we took around 10,000 fans, but it looked as though the whole of Swansea had made the trip. In fact, over the years I must have spoken to at least 20,000 people who said they were there that day!

The game itself started quite sluggishly, as I think the tension and occasion initially got to us. Then came a typical moment of magic from Leighton James. He curled a quite magnificent right-footer into the Preston net, which seemed to calm us down. We then got a second through Tommy Craig, and we went into the break feeling quite comfortable at 2–0 up, although we were very aware of the old saying that 2–0 is the most dangerous lead in football. During the interval, Tosh told us to keep playing as we were, but we still had to face another 45 nerve-racking minutes.

In the other dressing-room, the Preston manager Nobby Stiles must have read the riot act, because from the restart they tore into us, pulling a goal back straight away. I can still picture what happened shortly afterwards: a header from their centre-half Mick Baxter looked as if it was going in, only to thankfully graze the outside of the post. Then, with a few minutes to go, I made some ground down the right and passed inside to Robbie, who in turn slid the ball in to Charlo. He had come back into the side because of his ability to score crucial goals, and he finished off the move with a crisp left-foot drive. Final score 3–1, with promotion secured. There is no truth at all in the rumour that we were screaming at Charlo to stick the ball into the stand and that he mis-hit it and it ended up in the back of the net.

The goal vindicated Tosh's decision to play Charlo instead of John Mahoney, who had just recovered from an injury. Again, sentiment didn't cloud Tosh's judgement, as not only had they been brought up together in Cardiff, they were cousins. Tosh said at the time that if he managed for the next 50 years, he would not have to make a tougher decision than telling Josh he was not playing that day.

After the final whistle, the first player to be hugged was Dudley Lewis, a young local lad who had come in and replaced Leighton Phillips for the last 18 games or so of the season, producing performances that belied his tender age. When we eventually got back to the dressing-room, there was pandemonium and there were quite a few famous names from the sporting world there. Besides our directors, in attendance were Shanks, Wales manager Mike England, Gareth Edwards, in my view the greatest rugby player of all time, and even Nobby Stiles, who offered us his congratulations. Of course, the cameras and reporters were also there in abundance.

Amongst the euphoria, no one realised that Speedy had torn ligaments in the first half but had decided not to tell anyone. The fact that he played on showed his tremendous commitment to the cause.

After a couple of hours at the ground, we began the coach journey home with our wives and girlfriends for what was a memorable celebration. We stopped off at the Marriott Hotel in Liverpool, where amongst others Graeme Souness and Terry McDermott offered their congratulations. We stayed for a couple of hours before heading off for the final leg back to Swansea, with Wyndham leading the singalong. I asked Ann Stewart how she enjoyed the game and remember laughing when she said she'd spent the entire time sitting on the coach reading a book. Her husband, our keeper Dave Stewart, was extremely superstitious and had stopped her attending because he believed that every time she saw him play he was on the losing side. Whilst we were playing the most important game in the Swans' history, Ann Stewart was quietly reading a novel!

As you would imagine, the drinks flowed on the journey home, and we eventually pulled into the Vetch at about 2 a.m. There were hundreds of fans waiting to greet us, as well as Ante Rajković, who had missed the game through injury. The police escorted us off the coach, but we all wanted to carry on partying, so we ended up in The Bay View. The celebrations continued well into the next day, although we managed to get a few hours' sleep before we received a call from Tosh telling us to get up to Cardiff because BBC Wales were going to put out a promotion special. Unfortunately, Wyndham and Speedy were still in The Bay View and missed not only Tosh's call, but the recording as well. They could party, them boys!

After the celebrations had died down, there was a realisation of just what we had achieved. A dream had really come true, and within three months we would be stepping out to face the country's finest teams. I honestly could not recall how many players had come and gone since I first came to the club, but as it all began to sink in I was grateful there was one player still around to share it with me: the one and only Robbie James. When I first saw him playing in that trial match back in the early 1970s with Harry Griffiths, I had no idea what an impact he would later have on both me and the Swans. Even as a young boy, he had amazing strength and was so powerful, especially with that trademark burst down the right-hand side of the pitch. He was primarily a midfield player, which was his best position, but I played with him when he was magnificent as a striker, full-back or even centre-back. His left foot was adequate, but he could hit a ball with his right foot as hard and powerfully as any player I have ever seen. He scored goals with that right foot with blasts from 25 yards on a regular basis. When you add into the mix that he had great heading ability, was a good tackler and a fierce competitor, you had all the ingredients for a really fantastic player.

When I think of all the great players I played alongside with the Swans, Robbie was the best. Just after he made his debut, we played non-league Kettering in the FA Cup, who were managed at the time by 'Big' Ron Atkinson. Ron's brother Graham was a lump of a centre-half, and he and Robbie went in for a 50-50 ball, which Robbie won with a hard but fair tackle, resulting in Atkinson suffering a broken leg. Big Ron ran onto the pitch to confront Robbie, threatening to kill him. Harry Gregg stepped in between them, telling Big Ron that he would have to go through him first. To be honest, I know that

Robbie would not have shirked the confrontation if Harry hadn't intervened.

As well as being the best I ever played with, Robbie was also one of my best friends. He was really laid back, with a dry sense of humour, and he loved a night out with the lads. I will never forget the day he passed away. Robbie had taken over as player-manager of Llanelli Town, and I had spoken to him earlier in the day and arranged to have a drink with him after Llanelli's game down at Stebonheath Park against Porthcawl Town. I planned to speak to him again before the match but suffered a puncture on the way so did not arrive until it had already started. Midway through the first half, Robbie was challenged for the ball and then suddenly collapsed. At first, I thought it might have been ligament damage, but it soon became apparent that it was a lot more serious. Robbie was hardly ever injured, and even when he was he would just get up and carry on. I sensed something was seriously wrong.

The game was abandoned, and Robbie was rushed by ambulance to the nearby Prince Philip Hospital. I had to phone his wife, Karen, to tell her to come to the hospital as soon as she could. It was a horrible phone call to make. Robbie's parents were at the game, and their ashen faces told their own story. When all the family had gathered, the doctor gave them the news that Robbie had passed away. I was with ex-Swan Vic Gomersall, who was working for Llanelli, and as you can imagine we were stunned and shocked. It was a tragedy, first of all for his family, but also for his friends and an army of supporters. Robbie was only 40, and I am sure he would have, like me, returned to the Swans to play a part in the club's future.

Whenever we get together for reunions or special occasions, there is a very special person missing, and it will never be the same without Robbie. I know that his memory will live on through the many stories about him, and he will remain in the hearts of all Swans fans. One of the stories that best epitomises the regard in which Robbie was and is held comes from when he played for Cardiff City. After training at

Ninian Park, Robbie would return to Swansea to pick up his children from school still wearing his Cardiff kit. I think Robbie was the only person in Swansea who could have got away with that. A true legend in my and every member of the Jack Army's eyes!

The week after our promotion in 1981, another Swans legend, Wyndham, had his thoroughly deserved testimonial against Liverpool's 1974 FA Cup side, a reward for ten years' loyal service. Wyndham had seen it all in those years, including re-election to the Football League in 1975. He was also rewarded with a new one-year contract. Tosh, for his part, was offered a new five-year deal, perhaps because of the rumours continually linking him to the Anfield hot seat. To round off an incredible season, we lifted the Welsh Cup, beating Hereford 2–1 on aggregate, the first time we had won the competition since 1966.

Over the close season, there was once again a lot of player movement both in and out of the club. In came Dai Davies, returning to the Swans via Everton and Wrexham, to be joined by another ex-Evertonian, Bob Latchford, who was signed from Birmingham for £125,000. The Swans broke their transfer record with the £350,000 acquisition of Colin Irwin from Liverpool, and Max Thompson joined from Blackpool. Dave Rushbury was released and signed for Carlisle for £45,000, and Leighton Phillips joined Alan Mullery's Charlton Athletic for £25,000. When Leighton left, he told the tabloids what he thought of Tosh's man-management skills, an outburst that cost him a £100 fine, although Leighton maintained it was worth every penny.

On the management side, Doug Livermore, the Wales number two, was made first-team coach, Phil Boersma was appointed Tosh's assistant and Terry Medwin was switched to take charge of the youth team. There were rumours that Emlyn Hughes was coming on board as well, but these proved unfounded. Since Tosh's arrival, we had been known in some quarters as the 'Liverpool Old Boys'. Now, with Neil Robinson, Gary Stanley (who would sign a few weeks later), Bob and

Dai at the Vetch, we more closely resembled 'Everton Old Boys'.

With all the new players and a revamped management structure in place, it was time for pre-season training. We still did the running in the first couple of weeks, but Tosh made sure that the ball was never far away, unlike the old days at the Vetch when pre-season consisted of one run after another. I would like to have known what our record signing Colin Irwin would have made of the Mumbles run. I remember our then record signing Ronnie Rees's first attempt during my first season at the club. On the way back to the Vetch from Mumbles, the tide was out, so Ronnie thought he would take a short cut across the bay. Unfortunately for Ronnie, he got stuck in the sand, and Wyndham and I had to crawl in and pull him out.

One thing that did not change was the intensity with which we approached practice games. Training or not, there was no shirking of tackles. If Wyndham, Speedy or Robbie were my good friends, it counted for nothing in those games.

We all enjoyed the pre-season. There was a real buzz about the place, and the weeks passed quickly. And when the fixtures were announced, I was even more excited: our opening league fixture was to be Leeds at home. Preston was a huge game and a pretty nervous affair, but the game against Leeds United was equally significant for me personally. For us to play in the First Division against sides such as Leeds United was a tremendous achievement. And the fact that the first game of the season was against my former club made it extra special. I did not feel I had anything to prove to my old employers, but, as any player will tell you, I always wanted to do well against my old club.

I often felt quite nervous before big games, but before the Leeds match I remember visiting the toilet umpteen times and that my hands were visibly shaking. I thought back to Harry Griffiths' days and was hoping he would walk in with that old whisky bottle! I sat down and tried to pull myself together, but I knew as soon as I walked down the tunnel all the nerves and doubts would go away.

As I took part in the warm-up, I was greeted with the expected

The young Curtis family
(courtesy of the author)

With Philip at Madeline Street
(courtesy of the author)

My boys,
Ian and Gareth
(courtesy of the author)

Visiting the stables of Red Rum with Tosh and Charlo (© Harry Ormesher)

Signing for Leeds in 1979, with Jimmy Adamson and a despondent Tosh

Valetta 0, Leeds United 4, UEFA Cup, 19 August 1979. Kevin Hird, Brian Flynn, Peter Hampton and me on the bus from the hotel to the match already changed ready to play (© Sinister Pictures)

The all-sand pitch with little or no grass at the Gzira stadium in Valetta in August 1979 (© Sinister Pictures)

Wales v. Malta, 1979. New Leeds United teammates: me, Brian Flynn, Carl Harris and Byron Stevenson.

Goal of the month: Southampton 1, Leeds United 2, 1979 (© Bob Thomas Sports Photography)

All smiles for my return
to the Vetch, 1980
(© *South Wales Evening Post*)

Scoring for Swansea
against Cardiff at
Ninian Park. The
match ended 3–3

David Giles, Jeremy
Charles, Dudley Lewis,
Nigel Stevenson and I share
some bubbly after winning
promotion at Preston
(© *South Wales Evening Post*)

First Division, here we come

If the gates had been open, I'd have been straight down the Mumbles Road. Swansea 5, Leeds Utd 1

Me scoring a 'bullet' header from six inches against Sunderland at the Vetch

Me celebrating my goal against Ipswich Town in November 1981 (© Bob Thomas Sports Photography)

Swansea till I die!

Turning to the North Bank after scoring against Notts County (© *South Wales Evening Post*)

My last game for the Swans, against Bolton Wanderers, in 1990 at Vetch Field

In action for the Saints

My last farewell to the Vetch (© *South Wales Evening Post*)

Me and Meg at the Vetch
(© *South Wales Evening Post*)

The Wales Under-21 squad, 2008

With my wife in
Central Park, New
York, in 2008
(courtesy of the author)

chants of 'Reject' from the away fans, but I just smiled and cast my mind back to the Derby game the previous season when Leighton James had had to put up with the same thing and then smashed in a hat-trick.

On a balmy summer's day, I scored perhaps the most memorable goal of my entire career, the goal I have been reminded of so many times by supporters over the years. I can picture it as if it was yesterday. I loved playing out wide in front of the North Bank, and when Ante Rajković won the ball he immediately set me up in my favourite position. My first instinct was to attack the defender, who just happened to be the Leeds captain Trevor Cherry. I managed to force him back towards his own goal until we were at the edge of the penalty area. Then I just dropped my shoulder and cut back off my left foot before smashing a right-footer into the top corner of the net. I felt sheer joy, although I am a little embarrassed when I think back to my celebrations. If the gates had been open, I would have ended up down the Mumbles! It probably remains the greatest feeling I experienced in all the games I ever played. I know Tosh enjoyed the moment as well. When the ball hit the back of the net, he turned to Allan Clarke with a huge grin, gave him the thumbs up and said, 'Cheers, mate!' Clarke had questioned my ability, but thankfully Tosh had no doubts.

Our first few games in the top flight saw us give some good displays, with Bill Shankly giving us his endorsement, saying that we were not out of place in the division. After beating Spurs 2–1, with Robbie and me both scoring, we moved to third in the table behind West Ham and Ipswich.

Not long into the season, Leighton James celebrated his 400th league game with a 2–0 win against Alan Durban's Sunderland. The next game saw us lose 2–1 to Lokomotiv Leipzig, which meant we went out of Europe 3–1 on aggregate. This game included a particularly unwanted landmark for me, as I received my first red card as a professional, being sent off for retaliation after I was scythed down for the umpteenth time.

As we entered October, Tosh was not entirely happy with our performances. Dai Davies was going through a sticky patch, and the fans sometimes voiced their displeasure with him, mainly, I guess, because he replaced the crowd favourite Dave Stewart, who until the Leeds match had played in 57 consecutive games. Dai escaped Tosh's wrath, although the manager did place five experienced players on the transfer list, including Brian Attley, Tommy Craig, David Giles, Wyndham and Speedy. Speedy had only missed two games the previous season, so his inclusion was something of a shock. Even though Tosh had gone on record stating that Wyndham was the best pro he had ever worked with, there was no room for sentiment, as the manager proved yet again.

The first game in October saw us travel to Anfield for a match that proved to be a fitting memorial to Bill Shankly, who had passed away just before. Dai Davies was superb, but we only came away with a draw after letting a two-goal lead slip. Our confidence was given a boost after the game when it was announced that seven of us had been selected in the Wales squad: Leighton, Speedy, Dai, Gilo, Robbie, Charlo and me.

Things were not all rosy, though, as the club announced it had made an operating loss the previous season. I suppose the purse strings should have been tightened, but the chairman wanted the city to live the dream. So much so that he added Ray Kennedy to the squad for £160,000 from Liverpool the following month, taking the total spending to £850,000 in just eight months. At that time, Ray was the most-decorated player in the history of the game. With the Reds and Arsenal, he had a haul of trophies that included six league titles and three European Cups as well as winner's medals for the FA Cup, League Cup, Fairs Cup and UEFA Cup. He also won 17 England caps. He had an exceptional left foot and scored crucial goals, but Liverpool let him go as a gesture for his good service. It was some coup by the manager and chairman.

After our exploits for Wales, we found ourselves losing 4–0 to Man

City on the following Saturday, which was perhaps not surprising, as we had travelled to Russia and back. Tosh laid into us after that, saying that if we had a World Cup hangover, we could all sit on the bench. His threat helped to focus our minds and results improved over the next few games, so much so that after we beat Villa 2–1 at home on 15 December we topped the table, one point ahead of Man United. And there was good news for Speedy and Wyndham as well, as they were both taken off the transfer list, with Tosh telling Wyndham that there would always be a job for him as long as he was in charge.

We started off the new year with a 4–0 reverse at Liverpool in the FA Cup, although Tosh was not too disappointed, as we had a small squad and he wanted to focus on the league. He also said we should be judged in May.

Ray Kennedy's debut proved to be very special, as we beat Man United 2–0, with both Robbie and me scoring. Afterwards, Ray said that we had a genuine chance of winning the title, and I guess if anyone knew, it was him. The thing I remember best from that game, though, was the team talk. Tosh outlined his tactics and told Chris Marustik it was his job to mark Steve Coppell. The trouble with Muzzy was that he was not in awe of any of our opponents and asked Tosh who Coppell was because he had never heard of him!

As we entered February, Tosh decided to make changes to the squad, even though we were still in the mix. Out went Brian Attley to Derby and Gilo went to Palace in a swap for Ian Walsh. Harry Gregg was brought back to the club from Man United to coach our young keepers, Mike Hughes and Chris Sander. We ended the month beating Liverpool and completing the double over Arsenal. Almost four years to the day, we had lost to Rochdale; now we were in with a shout of landing the greatest prize in English football.

Tosh was still trying to find the right balance for the team, this time moving Tommy Craig out to Carlisle. It was 'lucky 13' in March when that many Swans players were selected for international duty.

Muzzy was called up for his first full cap, joining me, Leighton, Charlo, Robbie and Dai. Speedy, Dudley, Walshy and Jimmy Loveridge were called into the Under-21s, and Darren Gale, Gary Richards and Mike Hughes were in the youth squad. Before we played, Charlo suffered a serious injury that ruled him out for the rest of the season with a cartilage problem.

A small squad and international call-ups were clearly hampering our bid to stay with the leading pack. But with three wins on the spin, against West Brom, Southampton and Man City, we were defying the critics. The Saints game was special for me, because my goal won goal of the month on *Match of the Day*, my second success in the competition. Our good form was not going unnoticed, and there were rumours linking Tosh to the Liverpool job. Tosh dismissed them, saying that his family loved it in Swansea and that he was happy.

Towards the end of April, it became apparent that we would not win the title, so Tosh began to rotate the squad, giving the kids a chance in the league and playing his strongest team in the Welsh Cup. If we won it, we would qualify for the Cup-Winners' Cup, but we could also qualify for the UEFA Cup if we finished in the top six. The Cup-Winners' Cup was a tournament in which Welsh clubs had a proud tradition, including famous victories for Wrexham over Porto and Anderlecht, for Merthyr over Atalanta, and perhaps most famously for Cardiff over the mighty Real Madrid.

Wyndham made his First Division debut during May in the defeat at Spurs but got injured and cruelly missed out on any possible run in the first team. The season then fizzled out with four defeats in the last five games, including the finale at Villa Park, where we fielded five teenagers in the line-up: Sander, Lewis, Richards, Loveridge and Gale.

Some people argued that we had too many players away on international duty at any one time and that the travelling made us jaded. Tosh's gamble in the Welsh Cup proved successful, however, as we reached the two-legged final against Cardiff. After a goalless first leg at Ninian Park, we met again at the Vetch. Bob Latchford scored two as we came back from a goal down to win. The real 'hero', though, was Ante Rajković, who probably won us the game with his professional foul that stopped Phil Lythgoe as he burst clear with a potential opportunity for a one-on-one with our keeper. Ante duly received his marching orders, but his actions ensured that we won our second Welsh Cup under Tosh.

Compared with previous years, the 1982 close season was relatively quiet on the transfer front, with the only signing being Dean Saunders coming in on a full-time contract. We started our European campaign with a 3–0 home victory over Sporting Braga. Twelve months previously, Charlo had got our first goal in the First Division, now he scored our first goal in our first European victory. Unfortunately, I missed that, as I was still serving my European ban.

The away leg gave us an insight into what Continental football could be all about. Braga put us up in a substandard hotel, would not let us train on the pitch and moved the kick-off time. Tosh reported them to UEFA, and thankfully that type of thing does not happen too often these days. We still progressed to the next round, even though we lost 1–0, with Muzzy putting through his own net.

In the league, our form was not great, as we won two, drew one and lost four of our first seven games, although we entered September with a 4–0 demolition of Norwich, with Latch scoring a hat-trick. The season before, 24,000 fans had passed through the Vetch turnstiles for the match against Leeds, but for this game against the Canaries fewer than 12,000 turned up. Season-ticket sales were also down as the recession was beginning to bite particularly hard in South Wales.

There was further bad news the following week when the authorities imposed a transfer embargo on us because payments had not been made for the previous signings of Kennedy and Irwin. The Football League also ordered the Swans to cough up what we owed Everton for Gary Stanley, giving a deadline of seven months to complete payment.

A week later, only 5,000 turned up to watch the first leg of our second-round UEFA Cup-Winners' Cup tie with Sliema Wanderers, with the fans arguing that they could watch Barcelona for the same price. They, like me – I was still banned – missed a treat, as we won 12–0, giving us hope of beating Chelsea's record European aggregate score of 21–0. I was back for the second leg, which we won 5–0. I scored two, and then Tosh robbed me of a European hat-trick by subbing me, arguing that with such a small squad he could not run the risk of me getting injured. Unfortunately, Colin Irwin, our record signing, was injured, snapping his patella tendon. This injury was so bad that it later forced him into retirement. To make matters worse, the club did not receive all the insurance due to them because they had taken a risk on the premium. I guess it is just like insuring a £20,000 car but telling the insurers it is only worth £10,000 to save on payments. Colin was bought for £350,000, but the club did not value him as highly when insuring him.

Things were also going from bad to worse, with Tosh being charged with bringing the game into disrepute after he complained, perhaps too vociferously, about a penalty being retaken in the game against Watford, a charge that resulted in him being fined and banned from the touchline.

After some heavy defeats in the league, we faced Paris Saint-Germain in the third round of the Cup-Winners' Cup at the Vetch, with the club cutting ticket prices in a bid to win back the fans. After missing a host of chances, we were undone by a late sucker punch as they broke away to score the game's only goal. For the away leg, Tosh named himself sub, which meant he was able to sit in the dugout, finding a way around his ban. Our European adventure ended with a 3–0 aggregate defeat, which I guess was not a bad thing because of our small squad and our enforced transfer embargo. After all, the league was our major concern, especially as performances just before Christmas continued to be poor, which was reflected in the attendances dwindling to around 11,000.

Shortly after going out of the League Cup to Third Division Brentford, Tosh put Leighton James on the transfer list for £50,000, a figure that would have made little difference to our plight, as it was announced that we were over £2 million in debt by then. I was beginning to think that the club was jinxed, as we were stumbling from one crisis to another.

In the same period, I became embroiled in a club-versus-country row after I withdrew from the Wales squad after informing them that I could not play two games in a week. The Football Association of Wales would not accept my decision, so I had to turn up to be examined by Wales trainer Doug Livermore. This highlighted the farcical nature of the whole affair, as Doug was also the Swans trainer who had initially diagnosed that my knee was not up to the trip to Yugoslavia.

If we were hoping for a change of fortune as we entered the new year, we were in for a shock. Tosh lost his appeal against his four-month touchline ban, Leighton James was sold to fellow strugglers Sunderland, we were in the relegation zone and Ray Kennedy was stripped of the club captaincy, banned from playing and placed on the transfer list. I guess this was the first time in his career Tosh had experienced anything other than success. I would not go as far as to say that he had lost the plot, but some of his decision-making was becoming very erratic. The first time you knew you were not in his plans was when you turned up for training to find your kit had been moved to the away dressing-room, which the kids used. After this, there invariably followed a spell in the reserves, which is exactly what happened to Leighton just before he moved north. On one occasion, we turned up for training and the whole first-team squad was moved to the away dressing-room without a word of explanation from Tosh.

One of the reasons we had climbed the leagues was our togetherness; now our spirit seemed to have gone, and there was perhaps a lack of discipline at the club. There were rumours that Ray had been suspended because of his drinking and what Tosh perceived to be his low level of fitness. Ray had only made 11 appearances that season because of injury, and he did seem to struggle in training. I think Razor, as he was known, went along with the drinking stories because he had an idea that there might be another reason for his inconsistency. We later discovered that it was the onset of Parkinson's disease that was the real reason. At the height of the tension between them, Razor asked Tosh in front of everyone to place their medals on the table to prove who was the most successful.

After all the turmoil, Tosh decided to gamble on youth in the FA Cup against Norwich, a gamble that paid off, as we won 2–1, with youngsters Gary Richards and Darren Gale grabbing the goals. Darren also got the winner in the next game against Notts County, which meant we were going for three in a row away to Coventry. We grabbed a point in a 1–1 draw, but as we left the field the stadium announcer said over the Tannoy, 'The Swans may have won a point but not many friends after that display!' After the game, Tosh justified his game plan by telling the media it was up to the home team to entertain. That did not go down too well with the football purists on *Match of the Day*!

With the club in turmoil both on and off the field, Tosh decided to send us off to Marbella for a week, perhaps to relieve some of the pressure we were feeling. The roller-coaster ride that had become life at Swansea City was definitely beginning to take its toll. At the start of the season we were in five competitions, now we were in two.

Whilst we were away, Tosh took the unprecedented step of setting up meetings with the fans to discuss what was going on. Although there could be little disagreement amongst everybody associated with the club that if we carried on as we were we would be relegated, Tosh had to make do as best he could, because he could not bring anyone in. Since Tosh had arrived at the club, Malcolm Struel had always trusted his manager's judgement and backed him without question.

But with a squad of seventeen pros and ten or so juniors, the financial situation meant that those numbers could not be sustained. As a cost-cutting exercise, Max Thompson and Gary Stanley were placed on the transfer list.

On the field, Tosh was increasingly forced to play the youngsters, with Lewis, Richards, Gale and Loveridge starring in a 2–2 draw with Everton, although this positive performance didn't prevent us from dropping into the relegation places. The first game in March saw John Mahoney break his leg in three places, with another youngster by the name of Colin Pascoe coming on as a sub for his debut. In the same week, Bob Latchford turned down a potential move to Chelsea, which would have allowed the club to settle their debt with both Everton and Leeds.

Tosh then tried to get two players in, but the Football League blocked both loans and permanent signings. The manager was doing his best to turn things around, but his hands were tied both on and off the pitch. With all that was happening, I do not think that Bob Paisley, Brian Clough or Bobby Robson could have done a better job.

In March, Razor Ray Kennedy was still on the transfer list, as no one had showed any interest in signing him, perhaps frightened off by his wages, and he was soon joined by Dai Davies. Dai, like any keeper, made mistakes, but at times the abuse he received was vitriolic. Throughout my career, I never witnessed any other player suffer such abuse as he did.

Harry Gregg was also dismissed as the club tried to cut back on costs. After losing 4–1 to Man City, we drew with Sunderland and beat West Brom, leading Tosh to say that this team would still be around in the First Division in ten years. April saw us go six games without a win, picking up only two points, and it increasingly seemed that the next ten years were not going to be spent in the top flight.

With three games left, we gave ourselves a chance by beating Villa, but the other strugglers were also winning their games. Ray Kennedy, perhaps out of desperation, was given a place in the starting XI. It all proved in vain, as we lost the last two games to Man United and Notts Forest, which was somewhat ironic, as Tosh had said at the start of our first season at the top that these were the teams to emulate. For a relatively small club, we had punched above our weight against the big boys, but it proved to be not enough for us to avoid relegation. In a cruel twist of fate, a Leighton James-inspired Sunderland avoided the drop at our expense.

In the midst of a rumoured takeover by a Midlands businessman, we did at least win the Welsh Cup for a third consecutive time, with a two-legged win against Wrexham. Bob Latchford scored in every round, which took his tally to 34 for the season, some achievement considering the campaign we had.

As the season petered out, I felt demoralised, although not for one minute did I think that it would have ended the way it did, with relegation and the future of the club uncertain due to the mounting debt. However, if I thought things could not get any worse, I was sorely mistaken. Wyndham was released and joined Llanelli Town, and Robbie rejected the offer of a three-year deal and the promise of a testimonial. As was the case with me, Tosh had done all he could to stop Robbie going by offering him such a lucrative package. However, Robbie had proved that he could play at the highest level. With all due respect, though, I think he could have graced a bigger stage than Stoke City. After 400 games and 99 league goals, the Swans had got good value from him. The club asked for £250,000, but Robbie went for only £100,000, rising to a potential £160,000 after he had played 80 games, with the Swans also guaranteed 50 per cent of any sell-on fee.

The good news was that the transfer embargo was lifted, but only for the signing of players on free transfers. In came Jimmy Rimmer from Villa, Gary Chivers from Chelsea and Paul Maddy from Cardiff, with Max Thompson moving to Bournemouth. Jimmy, Ante and Bob also signed new contracts. These were perhaps not the big signings the fans had grown used to over the previous few years but surely the nucleus of a team that would push for a return to the First Division.

The 1983–84 pre-season started with a glut of meaningless friendlies. Gone, it seemed, were the days of glamorous games to whet the supporters' appetites. We did, however, face Magdeburg in the Cup-Winners' Cup, losing 2–1 over the two legs. Many positives came out of that tie, as both Ray Kennedy and Jimmy Rimmer were outstanding. On the basis of these performances, and with their experience, our optimism for a quick return to the top flight seemed realistic.

However, a few weeks into the new campaign and it was the same old story as the previous season. We lost to Sheffield Wednesday, managed by Howard Wilkinson, who was already developing his long-ball style, and Derby. A goalless home draw with Oldham was then played out in front of only 7,200 fans, our lowest attendance since Hartlepool in 1978.

With Charlo once again injured and with us at rock bottom, Tosh brought in his old mate Emlyn Hughes, otherwise known as 'Crazy Horse', on a three-month contract. A 36 year old with 625 games under his belt, Tosh was hoping Emlyn's experience would steady what appeared to be, even at that early stage of the campaign, a sinking ship. Hughes made his debut as captain at Huddersfield. Prior to the game, Bob Latchford asked to be placed on the transfer list. Leicester manager Gordon Milne agreed a fee for our striker, but an agreement couldn't be arranged with Bob over his wages.

Crazy Horse's first week was typical Swans, as players were put on the transfer list and then taken off again. This toing and froing was followed by yet another player exit. This time, Josh announced that the injury he had suffered seven months previously had forced him to retire. The club had done the right thing by Josh, keeping him on a monthly contract during his battle to come back from breaking his ankle in three places. Throughout his career, he made over 600 appearances and was a great guy to have in the dressing-room, as he always lifted our spirits. He was a model pro, a player's player, always putting the needs of others before his own, and there was many a time that he played with an injury, thinking of the team before his own welfare. He was also a patriotic Welshman and proud to pull on the red jersey. I thought Josh was indestructible and would go on for ever. I was pleased that the club gave him a position in the commercial department when he finished.

I'd thought things were bad when two of my best mates left during the close season, but they got worse when Muzzy asked for a transfer to further his career, which Tosh turned down, and then Malcolm Struel and Tom Phillips resigned from the board. With mounting debts and the Swans in a perilous position, Doug Sharpe, a director of three years, took over as chairman, promising to put forward a proposal to the bank that would ensure our future. Then, after missing half the previous season through injury, Charlo was also told he could go.

By October, we had gone almost twenty-six games without an away win, and I had missed seven matches through injury. By the end of the month, we were further adrift at the bottom of the division, but the off-field dramas meant this seemed insignificant. Swansea City were £1.5 million in debt, losing £10,000 a month, and the bank gave us just three weeks to raise £400,000 or they would bolt the gates. Sharpe wanted the 11 directors to donate half the amount between themselves and raise the other half by cutting wages and through an appeal to the fans. He also wanted to place the top-six earners on the transfer list – Ray Kennedy, Bob Latchford, Neil Robinson, Ian Walsh, Gary Stanley and me – adding that the club would listen to offers for any other members of the squad.

A few days later, Neil Robinson and I realised that the club had discovered another way of trying to raise some of this money. We were astounded when Tosh fined the two of us £100 for relieving ourselves in front of the public during a training session. We used to train on the old sports field of the Aluminium, Wire and Cable Company in Jersey Marine, which was at the side of the main road into Swansea off the M4. The ground was flanked by hedges, and we'd gone behind them, as we always did, to relieve ourselves while kneeling down, knowing full well that no one, not even our teammates, could see us. Tosh accused us of being undisciplined and unprofessional, but what offended us the most was that he accused us of peeing in front of schoolkids. To say that we peed in front of anyone was bad enough, but as parents ourselves we were dismayed, angry and hurt by Tosh's accusations. We were so incensed that we involved both the PFA and the Football League. Gordon Taylor was amazed that we had been fined, as we hadn't even been warned beforehand about our conduct. Also, the other players backed us up, and as it was in term time we had evidence that there were no kids there. Robbo was also fined a week's wages for losing his temper and swearing at Tosh. I guess this was another example of Tosh feeling the pressure, but after a meeting with the PFA, Tosh and the chairman, the whole episode died a death, much the same as the grass we peed on, I guess!

Not surprisingly, given the dressing-room unrest, we went out of the League Cup to Colchester. After the game, Sharpe, through our PFA representative Bob Latchford, asked the players to take a wage cut. Four days later, on the morning of our home game against Blackburn, Tosh sensationally left the club, by mutual consent according to the chairman. The boss was emotional and upset as he faced the press to say that he would not be seeking compensation for the remaining 18 months of his contract, rumoured to be in the region of £50,000 a year. As a goodwill gesture, he also donated a grand to the youngsters at the club. It was then announced that Ray Kennedy's contract, worth £30,000 a year, was also being paid up after he had made just 42 appearances. And, finally, Emlyn Hughes left to be replaced as captain by Jimmy Rimmer.

At the same time, the board also introduced a 'Save Our Swans' appeal, with the boxer Colin Jones as its patron, which in the first week raised £10,000. It went some way to saving the Swans, but I know a lot of marriages were put at risk, as some fans donated money that their wives had put aside for other things.

The council turned down the Swans' request for help, accusing the board of mismanagement and citing the fact that they had helped once before when they'd bought the ground, even though they'd got a £3-million asset for only £200,000. The council argued that the local toy-producing firm Mettoy's was also in trouble and that their workers were on far less money than we were.

The next two league games brought defeats against Chelsea and Middlesbrough, games I played in even though I was not fit. In the situation we were in, I would have played through any pain. Three days later, my Swans career was over for a second time, although I had no say in the matter, as I was shipped out to Southampton as part of the fire-sale. On the same day, Charlo took up Terry Venables' offer of a three-year contract at QPR. A little over two years previously, I had been in a team that contained six local boys (yes, I would call myself that!) for the game against Preston; now Leighton, Wyndham, Robbie, Charlo and I had for one reason or another all gone through the exit door. How would Speedy cope without us?

When I reflect on the Swans' time in the top flight, I would argue that the Leeds result gave us the impetus and momentum to carry on for the rest of that first season. We played some fantastic football and achieved some great results, beating Liverpool, the league title winners, Spurs, the FA Cup winners, Aston Villa, the European Cup winners and Ipswich Town, the European Cup-Winners' Cup winners. The list of teams we beat also includes Arsenal, who we did the double over, Man United and Man City. The Leeds United game was the highlight that season but beating Ipswich Town 3–2 at Portman Road ran it a close second. They were an excellent team that included Paul Mariner, Terry Butcher, Mick Mills and the two Dutchmen, Frans Thyssen and Arnold Mühren, but goals from Gary

Stanley and Bob Latchford and probably my best goal of the season saw us home in a thriller.

We did not particularly distinguish ourselves in Europe, but I do remember some funny incidents against Paris Saint-Germain. The first leg was at home, and Tosh, who was accustomed to some magnificent European nights at Anfield, built up the game as being a great experience and potentially the highlight of our careers. We were, therefore, highly motivated and could not wait to get at our French opponents, arriving at the Vetch a little earlier than normal to sample the atmosphere. Unfortunately, the gates all around the ground were locked when we arrived. Harold the groundsman had just nipped up to the town centre. Tosh was livid, which meant we were all afraid to laugh, but I guess it proved that the Swans were not quite ready for European glory just yet!

For the second leg two weeks later, we chartered a flight to Paris for the players, staff, directors and some supporters. Unfortunately, we lost the game, and when we arrived at the airport we were told our return flight would have to be delayed because of dense fog. Disappointment soon turned to mischief when one of the supporters by the name of Mike Sullivan managed to organise a courtesy bus to take us into the centre of Paris to sample its delights! A few of the fans had been to the French capital before and knew where to take us. We had a fantastic night, and the pain of defeat became a blur as the drinks flowed. Tosh did not realise we had been out, and thankfully everyone returned safely to the airport. This bonding session proved invaluable because we embarked on a long unbeaten run in the league afterwards.

Whereas the first year went like a dream in the top flight, unfortunately the same cannot be said for our second season. It is really difficult to pinpoint one major reason why it all changed so dramatically. There was probably a little bit of second-season syndrome, when the opposition tend to work you out. It also became apparent very quickly that we were not on a solid foundation financially.

During our second season, I also struggled with a niggling injury, which I picked up against Norwich City in the first week when I took a bang on my left knee. This restricted my movement for a large part of the campaign and eventually forced me to have an operation, which meant I missed quite a few games.

There was also a breakdown in the relationship between Tosh and some of the more senior players, including me. At the start of Tosh's reign, he brought in players who would enhance the team, such as Cally and Smithy. However, in our two seasons in the top flight, some of us perhaps thought that Tosh brought in players who did not add anything to the side. No disrespect to the likes of Gary Stanley, but he really was no better than Neil Robinson or Wyndham. Tosh liked to play a brand of exciting and attacking football whenever possible, and this sometimes affected the balance of the side. He would always try to accommodate the flair players, such as Leighton, Robbie, Charlo and Bob, which meant that he sometimes required other players to play out of position.

A combination of all these factors meant that we did not seem to have the spirit of old and results went against us. When our demotion was finally confirmed, it was a sad ending to what had been a fairy-tale journey. It has been said that Swansea City's further demise in later years was down to the time we spent in the old First Division, and it can be argued that it has taken us all these years to recover. However, it was still a remarkable journey, and despite the ending it was the most enjoyable period of my career. And I'm sure many fans would agree that it was one of the most exciting times to support the team.

Fast forward 25 years, and I have a feeling of déjà vu. As the Swans finished eighth on their return to the second tier of English football, hopes are high that the club can continue to challenge for a place in the Premier League, and comparisons between Tosh and Roberto Martínez were inevitable. Tosh has had an excellent career. Anyone who has managed Real Madrid twice, plus been a boss in Portugal, Italy, France, Turkey and in Spain with other clubs, as well as managing at international level, deserves all the plaudits you can give. Tosh developed into a world-class coach, especially on the Continent, where the presence of a sporting director perhaps allowed him to focus primarily on team affairs. Roberto, as with Tosh, started out in management at a young age, and they both have a great aura. It is a special quality that you find in all the top people, be it in football, business or politics, and the two former Swans managers have it in abundance. They are both single-minded in their approach and know exactly what they want to achieve. It was easier for me to see Roberto's qualities. As a member of the Swans coaching staff, I could see his methods up close, whereas under Tosh it was more a case of me playing my own game, even though he guided me along. Both are tactically excellent and have imaginative and innovative ideas on how their teams should play. Roberto likes to play intricate patterns, based on a sound defence in which the defenders are comfortable on the ball. In comparison, Tosh would regularly change systems, including sometimes playing three at the back and sometimes three up top. While attractive football is a big feature of both men's sides, especially Roberto's, the ability to work hard and win the ball back when the opposition has it is also vital.

Both teams have played wonderful football, and comparisons are inevitable when it comes to past and present teams and players. I would not like to select a combined side, because it would prove impossible. How could you not pick Leon Britton, Ferrie Bodde and Àngel Rangel in any Swans team from any era? Likewise, how could you leave out Leighton and Robbie James, Ante Rajković or Jimmy Hadžiabdić? Older generations of supporters would obviously pick Ivor Allchurch, our greatest ever Swan, plus Mel Charles, Terry Medwin, Cliff Jones and Mel Nurse. My uncle, Roy Paul, and Herbie Williams would also need to have a place found for them, along with Lee Trundle. All I know is that if I had a magic wand to help me select the greatest-ever Swans XI, I would have a team that would regularly challenge for the Premier League and beyond. Now who would the manager be?

7

PATIENCE OF A SAINT

On 30 November 1983, I was sold to Southampton for £70,000. They were then a team who seemed to be on the threshold of breaking through to challenge the Merseyside dominance and were at that time sixth in the First Division. On paper, the move seemed ideal for me. Lawrie McMenemy, their manager, had been progressively building on the Saints' FA Cup win in 1976 and had signed some big names to complement the club's traditional reputation for developing good home-grown youngsters. However, I had been happy at the Swans, and with no disrespect to Southampton or their fans, I never really wanted to leave Swansea: the club or the city. (In fact, I never actually asked for a transfer at any of the clubs I played for.)

If it had just been about my career, I would have probably more readily accepted the move, but our family had just been given the devastating news that my mother had cancer, which meant that I was even more reluctant to leave South Wales. We were a close family, and I wanted to be as near as possible to help support my mother and the rest of the family through what was obviously a difficult period. As a professional footballer, I accepted that the move to Southampton would be of great financial necessity to the Swans, because the club was on the verge of going bankrupt, but from a personal perspective I didn't want to be three hours' drive from my family. My parents had always been fully supportive of my career, and even at this very stressful time they told me that I should go to Southampton and make a real go of it. It was typical of my mum that she should think of her family before herself, and it is difficult to describe the mix of emotions I was going through at the time as I contemplated the move to the south coast.

When I arrived at Southampton, Lawrie McMenemy and the coaching staff made a real effort to help me fit in, and I was very grateful for the support that they gave me. I think another factor that helped me to settle more quickly was that Southampton was a friendly club with a family atmosphere, and the Dell was very reminiscent of the Vetch, with the terraces close to the pitch.

I had also heard a lot of positive things about the Saints manager, and these were certainly reinforced by my initial dealings with him. He told me that he really wanted me to be a part of what he was building at the club and that he had first tried to sign me nearly eight years previously but the then Swansea coaching team of Harry Griffiths and Harry Gregg had turned down his offer. McMenemy was very complimentary about my career and told me that he had followed my progress over the years with keen interest. He said that as the Swans were so strapped for cash, the Saints were getting me for a bargain and that he was sure that I would do well at the club. He had a way of making you feel very much part of the set-up and motivating you to want to do well for him. Even when things were not going so well on the pitch for you as a player, he was always approachable and willing to offer advice and encouragement on how you could improve and you always felt that he treated you with respect. This was just as well, as my first season with the Saints was probably as disappointing for McMenemy as it was for me.

The club had undergone somewhat of a transition since the famous cup-final victory over Manchester United under the captaincy of

Wales full-back Peter Rodrigues, the first Welshman to captain a winning team since Uncle Roy 20 years earlier. In the early 1970s, Southampton was a club with a tradition of developing a majority of its own players from the local area, supplemented with old pros coming to the end of their careers. However, by the early 1980s, as well as continuing to encourage local talent into the first team, McMenemy had been able to attract much higher-profile players, including Alan Ball and Kevin Keegan, to the club. It was very much the same when I joined, as promising youngsters such as Mark Wright, Steve Moran, Danny Wallace and Steve Williams were complemented by big-name stars such as Peter Shilton, Mick Mills and Frank Worthington.

In the same week that I joined the club, Swansea also sold Jeremy Charles to QPR for £85,000, and Mark Dennis joined the Saints from Birmingham. Mark had a reputation as being one of the game's most physical players, which perhaps partly contributed to him being sent off 12 times in his career. During his time with Southampton, I rated him as one of the top full-backs in the country, and I think he would have probably won many England caps if it hadn't been for the negative press coverage his image on and off the field brought him.

I made my Saints debut as a striker at the Dell in a 3–1 victory over Stoke three days after signing for the club. In the next two games, I kept my place as we held the team I had followed as a boy, Spurs, to a goalless draw at White Hart Lane and then beat Birmingham 2–1 at home. As we moved on to Upton Park to face West Ham on Boxing Day, I felt that I had done quite well to win a place in a very good side that was challenging at the top of the First Division.

It was during the second half of the 1–0 victory over the Hammers when I pulled my hamstring that things started to go wrong for me. The injury is obviously quite a common one for footballers and was probably a regular occurrence in matches up and down the country on that cold December afternoon. However, it was not the nature of the injury but the timing of it that was so damaging for my progress at the club. If you ask any professional footballer, they will tell you there is never a good time to be injured, but the two worst times are when you join a new club or when the team goes on a winning run without you. For me, both these scenarios occurred at the same time, and for a variety of reasons it was to be four months before I played for the first team again.

Looking back, the hamstring pull was perhaps inevitable, as I had been carrying a niggling injury when I signed for the Saints and was never really fully match fit. In my last two months at the Swans, I really needed to take a few weeks off to rest a leg strain, but the manager was desperate for me to play, and the situation wasn't helped by the club having no full-time physio at that time because of the cash crisis. Also, I was so keen to press my claims for a first-team place at the Dell, there was no way I was going to ask them for any time off training to rest, and I probably ended up pushing myself too hard in those first few weeks on the south coast rather than trying to acclimatise more sensibly to the extra pace and fitness demanded at the higher level.

As I was recovering from my injury, Steve Moran replaced me and grabbed his opportunity to impress by scoring nine times in the next seven games. It was clear that Steve had established himself up front, and this meant that Frank Worthington, Danny Wallace and I were going to be competing for the right to partner him. It is worth remembering also that this was a time when teams were only allowed to name one substitute, which inevitably made competition for places even harder. The team were playing well and displaying impressive league form, and they also made progress in the FA Cup, with excellent away victories over Nottingham Forest and at a very hostile Fratton Park against Portsmouth in the fifth round.

In early February, my mum passed away, and I immediately travelled home to be with my family. I have to say that the manager and staff at the club were all very supportive at what was obviously a very sad time for me and allowed me two weeks off. In fact, they were very understanding throughout my mum's illness, especially as I spent a lot of time travelling back to the Rhondda from Southampton.

When I returned to the club, I felt it might be difficult to motivate myself for the psychological and physical challenge of regaining my place in the first team. But it was my job as a professional footballer to give Southampton my best effort, as my parents had taught Phillip and me that we should never give less than 100 per cent effort at whatever we did. The task of getting back into the side, however, wasn't going to be an easy one, as under McMenemy's guidance the team were flying in both the league and FA Cup. A 2–0 victory over Liverpool at the Dell in the middle of March put us in fourth, eight points behind the Anfield club and nine points behind leaders Manchester United. An emphatic 5–1 replay win over Sheffield Wednesday had also put the team in striking distance of a second FA Cup-final appearance at Wembley.

The situation for me was a little bit surreal, as whilst the on-field success had created a real buzz around the club and within the city, I still felt a little bit on the periphery of events, despite the manager's reassurances. Having played in four consecutive games after signing for the club, I hadn't played in the first team for nearly four months. I gave my all in training and was determined to impress in my first reserve game back away at Watford. You can imagine how exasperated I was when, early in the match, I injured the same knee that had given me so many problems at Leeds. As I missed another fortnight's vital training, parallels with my time at Elland Road were beginning to cross my mind.

Even though I am generally a very positive person, I did begin to have some doubts and became a little worried that I might find myself frozen out of the first team more permanently at the Dell. I have to say, though, that at this time the coaching staff at the Dell were absolutely brilliant. I know that in many clubs an injured player is often seen as an inconvenience by managers and coaches, and the attitude of 'out of sight, out of mind' is often ruthlessly adopted, but my experience under McMenemy's coaching staff was completely different. Both Lew Chatterley and John Mortimer were great and would always take time out after training to give a few quiet words of encouragement or put the proverbial arm around my shoulders to tell me that I was still in the boss's thoughts and that I'd be back in the first team before I knew it. I have to say that their tactics were spot on, as I have always responded more to the 'heart to heart' style of management than the 'kick up the backside' approach.

Unfortunately, after Lew left the club to follow Lawrie to Sunderland, I can't say I enjoyed the same positive experience under the management and coaching team of Chris Nichol, when out of sight definitely did mean out of mind. Lew later returned to the Dell, where he was briefly caretaker manager in the mid-1990s, before retraining to become a teacher, and I believe he's now a coach at Winchester School. Going by my experience working with Lew, they are very lucky students, as he is an excellent coach and a really nice guy.

Whilst I spent yet more time on the physio's table, the first-team squad were preparing for the vital semi-final clash with Everton on 14 April at Highbury. The other semi had seen Plymouth and Watford come out of the hat together, so the winners of the Highbury semi were firm favourites to lift the cup. I watched the game from the stands, and it would be fair to say that the Saints were unlucky not to reach the final. If it hadn't have been for Big Nev in the Everton goal, who was outstanding, we probably would have made it to Wembley. After missing a string of good chances in the 90 minutes, the 'sting in the tail' came in extra time, as so often happens, when Adrian Heath scored the game's only goal in the 117th minute.

In a quirk of the fixture list, Everton were to be the visitors at the Dell only three days later. Lawrie McMenemy had promised the fans that the team wouldn't let the FA Cup disappointment get to them and that they would continue fighting until the end of the season in search of one of the vital European places. The team responded magnificently to our manager's rallying cry, and in a dramatic run we won six and drew three of the last nine games. These results included a revenge 2–1 defeat of Everton, an 8–2 mauling of Coventry and a 5–0 drubbing of Spurs.

During the second half of the victory over Everton, I came on as a sub to play my first game since Boxing Day. I started the next two games, a victory over West Ham and a draw with Watford, as a midfield replacement for the injured Steve Williams. On Saturday, 28 April, I was selected to play ahead of the now recovered Williams and was beginning to at last feel part of the first-team set-up, especially as we raced to a 4–1 half-time lead over Coventry. I was really enjoying myself in what was a relatively unaccustomed central-midfield role when in the 63rd minute my injury jinx returned again. I went in for a routine 50-50 challenge with Coventry's Nick Platnauer and took a knock to my ribs and came off as a precaution. When I went for an X-ray, it was revealed that I had actually cracked a rib and that I would be ruled out for the last five games of the season. I really couldn't believe how much bad luck I was having that season in terms of niggling injuries, and it tested to what extent I had the patience of a saint!

Whilst I sat out the last few games, the team continued their good form, and we eventually finished as runners-up in the league, only three points behind the champions Liverpool. It had been a great effort and marked the highest league finish that the Saints had ever achieved. It was even more credit to the Southampton squad that we had pushed Liverpool all the way to the title, as the Merseyside club had in recent years dominated domestic football, with this being their fifth title in six seasons. The Liverpool squad also contained a host of seasoned internationals and familiar household names, including Alan Hansen, Kenny Dalglish, Graeme Souness, John Wark, Ian Rush, Mark Lawrenson, Steve Nicol and Ronnie Whelan. The fact that Southampton, with its small squad and financial constraints, partly brought about by crowds of fewer than 20,000, could challenge a team that went on to win a further three titles in the 1980s was of great credit to Lawrie McMenemy.

Whilst the club had enjoyed its most successful season ever – other than 1976, of course – it was probably one of the most unsuccessful and frustrating of my own career. It had been a very difficult year to say the least, and I can't say I was sorry to see the back of the 1983–84 campaign. However, I was and still am a great believer in the importance of a good pre-season and felt that if I could get a good six weeks' training in, I could get myself back into the first-team frame.

The major personnel change for the Saints in the close season came in the form of former Leeds and Man United striker Joe Jordan, who arrived at the club as Frank Worthington left to join Brighton, which was to be his eighth of eleven league clubs in total. Both Joe and Frank had made their names as successful strikers in the top flight in the 1970s but were very different players and personalities. When he arrived at the Dell, Frank announced to everybody who would listen that his training regime would consist of a little bit of five-a-side and the occasional bit of shooting practice. In contrast, Joe Jordan was one of the most professional footballers I ever met. During his time at AC Milan in the early 1980s, he fully absorbed the Italians' professional approach to training and would be out on the pitch 30 minutes before the rest of the squad and leave 30 minutes after everybody else had finished training. Joe was a really lovely guy off the pitch, but on it he was as 'hard as nails', and you always hoped you were on his side in training.

During the 1984 pre-season, a training match took place behind closed doors at the Dell. Naturally, with only a few weeks to go before the new season, everybody was out to impress. Straight from the kick-off, our centre-back Kevin Bond went through the back of Joe and gave him a real whack. There was an awkward silence as Joe dusted himself off and slowly got back to his feet. Two minutes later, our side won a corner, which was gathered by Peter Shilton. As he cleared up field, everybody turned back to see a completely poleaxed Kevin Bond flat out in the box. Nothing was said, and the game continued without Kevin, but after that our defenders were much more careful about taking liberties with Joe in training matches or five-a-side.

At the beginning of the season, Lawrie, like any good manager, gave us his review of the previous season and set out his expectations and goals for the forthcoming campaign. He reiterated to me that he had every faith in my abilities and that if I could keep injury free, I would always be in contention for a first-team place.

The 1984–85 season began disappointingly, and after a 3–1 defeat against Sunderland at Roker Park we didn't win any of the first five games and found ourselves bottom of the table. At least I had started the season more positively than I had ended the previous one, and I was a playing substitute in each of the first four games. The fifth game of the season, a 1–1 draw with Luton, was a bit of a watershed in my time at the Dell. It not only marked my first goal for the club, but it was also the start of the first sustained period in which I was able to hold down a regular first-team place. In a repeat of the previous season's good form, we then went on an 18-match domestic unbeaten run, our only defeat being in the second leg of the UEFA cup tie with SV Hamburg. My appearance in the goalless home leg at the Dell meant that I was fortunate enough to have participated in European competition with all four teams I played for. I had played in the Cup-Winners' Cup with Swansea, a competition in which I was also later to represent Cardiff, and in the UEFA Cup with both the Saints and Leeds. It was obviously a blow to be knocked out at the first-round stage, but Hamburg was probably one of the toughest draws we could have had, given that two years earlier they had won the European Cup, defeating the Italian giants Juventus in the final.

Our unbeaten run finally came to an end on 12 December when we lost a League Cup replay 4–0 to QPR on their controversial plastic pitch. Although we had lost at Loftus Road by the same score the previous season, I'm not sure it was anything more than coincidence, as later that season we reversed the result by beating them by the same scoreline in the league. The plastic pitches that QPR and Luton had at that time were terrible, and the bounce was very erratic. The artificial pitches of today are very advanced compared to those 1980s plastic pitches, but I can't say I am a real fan of artificial pitches for competitive fixtures, and I can see why England were so unhappy when they had to play Russia on a plastic pitch in October 2007 and lost 2–1.

I was really happy with my contribution during this period, and apart from the second leg against Hamburg I had played in every game. It gave me particular pleasure that I was selected by the manager in a more central-midfield position, which was a completely different role for me, and I also managed to score some valuable goals. I had always played up front or out wide, so it was a new experience for me in the centre of the park, and to play there consistently in a successful First Division team was very rewarding. I especially enjoyed playing in this new role at the Dell, where we had a great record and were encouraged to play a high-tempo, attacking style of game. It probably gave me most satisfaction that after the disappointment of my time with Leeds and the first season with the Saints, I proved I could play consistently and injury free at that level. Mike England made me even happier by recalling me to the Welsh squad at that time as we challenged for a place at the World Cup finals in Mexico.

Despite our excellent run, which had taken us from the bottom of the league to fifth place behind Everton, storm clouds were gathering over the club. Just as Lawrie McMenemy began to assemble a squad that he thought could challenge the dominance of Liverpool and Everton in domestic football, star players Steve Williams and Mark Wright demanded transfers, as they believed they could command higher wages elsewhere. The relationship between McMenemy and Wright became very strained, and after one particularly heated exchange it was alleged that the Saints manager ended up in the team bath. When the boss was questioned on the incident by the press, he replied dryly that he 'enjoyed taking a bath every day'.

A 1–0 win over Ipswich on 1 December was a club record 13th match unbeaten, which was stretched to 14 games when we beat Arsenal 1–0 at the Dell in the next fixture. It was during the game against the Gunners that I scored probably my best goal for the Saints. I received the ball from a throw-in, turned away from my marker and was delighted when a 25-yard curler from outside the box flew into John Lukic's net. I'm not sure why, but two of my favourite goals were scored when my former Leeds colleague was in the opposition goal!

Sport, and in particular football, has a habit of bringing you back down to earth very quickly, and our unbeaten run ended the next week when we lost two games in three days, to QPR in the cup and Coventry in the league. It's difficult to say how much impact the transfer saga of Wright and Williams had on the team's performances, but after the arguments developed between the two 'want away' stars we never really matched the autumn form during the remainder of the season, so I think it certainly must have had some effect and was perhaps more significant than we thought at the time.

Mark Wright went on a one-man strike and refused to train, and I don't think his relationship with the manager was much improved when he told his side of the story to a Sunday tabloid. I travel a lot with my new jobs with Wales and the Swans and like to read the autobiographies of past players, but I feel strongly that sportsmen and women should keep their memoirs and columns until after they retire. There have been too many instances in recent years when people still involved in their sporting fields have written memoirs that have stirred controversy. David O'Leary and Glenn Hoddle come to mind, as does the fallout caused in my native Wales by rugby star Gavin Henson's book in 2005.

The situation was no less strained with Williams, who was in limbo, having not been picked since early November after having a transfer request turned down when Arsenal refused to match the Saints' asking price. The situation resolved itself by the new year, as Williams was transferred to Arsenal for £500,000, and Wright patched up his differences with the manager and ended his strike. Perhaps the biggest potential impact that these events had was to sow doubts in the mind of Lawrie McMenemy about the ability of Southampton as a club to keep its better players and whether he really had the full backing of the board in being able to match the potential wages that could be offered by the so-called glamour clubs such as Arsenal.

After the December slump, when we lost three of our four league games and exited the League Cup, our form did pick up in the new year, although it never really managed to rise to the heights of the previous season. Our record in the second half of the campaign was reasonable, as we won eleven, drew four and lost six games in the league. In the FA Cup, there was no repeat of the previous season's success, as we lost at home to Barnsley in the fifth round, then managed by ex-Leeds and Everton star Bobby Collins.

On 2 April, I missed only my second league game of the season, a 1–0 win over Luton, after straining a hamstring. I think that I was so keen to get back into the team that I started to train too early, ended up aggravating the injury and missed most of the last few weeks of the season. I did recover in time to come on as a half-time substitute in the crucial last game of the season when we hosted Liverpool at the Dell. In Mick Mills' last career game, a 1–1 draw was good enough to seal fifth place and another shot at Europe, although we were never actually able to take up our place in the UEFA cup the following season as a result of the fallout from the Heysel stadium disaster. Mick was a model pro who excelled for both Ipswich and Saints, playing to a consistently high standard in over 700 games and winning 42 caps for England. He was always a thoughtful player and talked a lot of sense about the game in a very calm and positive manner. I always thought that he would make a very successful manager or coach and was quite surprised that after four years with Stoke and a short spell as manager of Colchester he didn't continue down the management path.

Despite the disastrous start to the campaign, a fifth-place finish and a European spot could be seen as success and kept the club amongst the elite of domestic football. When I reflect on that season, I was happy to have played regularly, especially in what was for me a new position in the centre of the park. I played in over forty games and scored six goals from midfield, which made me feel that I had contributed to the club's success. Considering how the previous season had gone, I was really happy to have remained fit and to have played so many first-team games. I hoped that my efforts during the 1984–85 season had gone some way towards rewarding the faith that Lawrie McMenemy had shown in me during my injury-ridden first season. I believed that I could build upon this progress the following season and continue to keep my place in the first-team squad. However, during the close season the worst-case scenario for me occurred as McMenemy sensationally quit the club.

In early June, the Southampton manager announced that he was leaving the club after over 12 years in charge. McMenemy had never played professionally, having quit at a young age after smashing his knee whilst playing in a game while he was in the army. He had started his managing career in his native north-east with non-league Gateshead before successful spells in charge of Doncaster and Grimsby, arriving at the Dell in 1973. During his time on the south coast, he had transformed the Saints from a small club with ambitions of surviving in the top flight to one that annually challenged for Europe. As well as guiding Southampton to a regular place in the top ten of the league, he had of course famously won the 1976 FA Cup as well as leading the club to the 1979 League Cup final, when they were runners-up.

CURT

I found McMenemy to be an excellent manager, although I wouldn't have described him as a great coach, as he wasn't really what you would call a tracksuit manager. He would leave most of the actual training to his coaches, and you would rarely see him at the training pitch between Monday and Friday. However, on a one-to-one basis, he was fantastic and commanded respect with his firm but fair manner, and he always made me feel an integral part of his plans, even when I was out of the team for quite a long period during my first season at the club. Like any good manager, he also had his tough side, as demonstrated by his unwillingness to tolerate what he saw as the undisciplined behaviour of Mark Wright and Steve Williams. He could administer an almighty bollocking to players who stepped out of line while never seeming to alienate them, which is always a difficult task.

A typical example was McMenemy's handling of a young apprentice called Mark Whitlock, who after coming runner-up in a yard-of-ale contest in his local pub inadvertently found his photo gracing the back pages of the local newspaper under the headline 'Young Saints Star Runner-up in Pub Olympics'. Naturally, the boss got to hear about it, and Mark was dragged in to explain his actions. After lengthy admonishment about drinking and bad publicity, Mark feared the worst as McMenemy stated that above all he had brought the club's name into disrepute. As the young apprentice stared at the ground, the Saints boss stated that on no account should any Saints player be satisfied with being a runner-up in any competition they entered. McMenemy had done his job, telling off the young player, but had also won the youngster's respect by showing he could see the funny side. Mark went on to play over 60 times for the first team before leaving for Bournemouth shortly after McMenemy himself had left.

I had been happy under his management, as I knew that despite my injury-ravaged first year at the club he rated me as a player, and he picked me regularly in my second season.

The new manager was to be former Aston Villa and Saints favourite Chris Nichol, and right from the start I got the impression that I wasn't his sort of player. Football relationships are like those in any other work environment: sometimes people prefer to employ or work with one person over another without there seeming to be much rhyme or reason to it. I think it was the same for me working under Nichol. I never had any cross words or arguments with him, and, in fact, I don't really remember having many, if any, conversations with him when I wasn't in the first-team squad.

I got the feeling that it was going to be difficult to become a regular in his side when I wasn't selected for any of the pre-season games, Nichol preferring Jimmy Case and Andy Townsend in the midfield position I had been occupying the previous season. Andy and Jimmy were both outstanding players, but it seemed to me that Nichol preferred the more physical style of play they seemed to offer. There were certainly some murmurings of discontent amongst the Saints fans, who were used to and appreciated a more attacking and attractive brand of football from their team. However, I must say that the club's supporters were very loyal and still filled the ground every week to cheer on their team, even if they didn't fully endorse the team's style of play during that period.

I wasn't selected for the opening fixture, a 1–1 draw at home to Newcastle, but was picked in the next game at Highbury after several players, including Jimmy Case and Joe Jordan, got injured. Joe's knee injury was a serious one and kept him out for most of the remainder of the season, which was a big blow to the team. I was really interested when reading his autobiography that Joe said that Nichol also hardly spoke to him in all the time he was injured and away from the first-team scene.

Despite playing in the next ten league games, I just didn't get the vibe that Nichol was going to pick me regularly if he had a full squad to choose from, and the fact that he signed Glenn Cockerill from Luton for £200,000 probably reinforced these feelings. In mid-October, I wasn't selected for the away trip to face Luton at Kenilworth Road. This was probably as good a game as any to miss, as we were hammered 7–0. After such a humiliation, I was surprised not to be recalled to the first-team squad, and I think at that stage I knew the writing was on the wall. It was. I never played in the league for the first team again. In five suffocating and frustrating months, I only played three more first-team games, twice in the League Cup, one a win over Birmingham and the other a draw with Arsenal, and in an FA Cup third-round win over Middlesbrough.

By March 1986, I hadn't played a league game since 12 October at Anfield so snapped up the offer of a loan spell with Stoke and a change of scenery. Being a footballer is perceived as being a glamorous profession, and I wouldn't deny that it can be very rewarding when things are going well. However, when you are stuck in the reserves for months on end, it can test the patience and motivation of the most even-tempered player. Unlike under the previous regime, it seemed as though you were completely out of the picture if you were not in the first-team set-up. The experience made me determined that if I ever became a coach or manager I would ensure, as much as possible, that a player who found himself out of the first-team set-up would never feel ignored or undervalued.

One happy memory I do have of that period was playing in a friendly against Manchester United. The game was a fund-raiser played in front of over 20,000 fans to try to help the Swans out of their dire financial crisis. I played for my old team and felt quite emotional when the Swansea fans chanted 'We want Curt' after I scored a goal, suggesting to the management that the club should re-sign me. However, this was never an option. With debts of nearly £1 million, the club was issued with an embargo that meant they couldn't sign players, even on loan deals.

Whilst I was on loan with Stoke, the Saints reached their second FA Cup semi-final in three years. Unfortunately, there was to be heartache again, with the team suffering a 2–0 reverse to Liverpool after extra time. Unlike two years before, it wasn't bad luck, and this time only an outstanding performance from Peter Shilton in the Southampton goal kept the team in it for so long.

Shilton was a fantastic keeper. He was a commanding presence in goal during practice matches, and you really had to work to score past him. However, he very much kept himself to himself during the time I was at the club, and I can't say I really got to know him well. I was also a little surprised that given the serious nature of the injury I suffered when I collided with him in 1980, he never actually mentioned the incident once during the time we played together at the Dell. I also think that some of the players might have got the feeling that because of his reputation and status in the game, his training schedule was sometimes a little more flexible than the majority of the rest of the squad.

At the end of the 1985–86 league season, there was no repeat of previous seasons' successes, as we finished a disappointing 14th. My contract was up, and I felt that it was time for me and the club to part ways.

If you look at the stats of my time at the Dell, I only played fifty or so league games in three seasons, so my time there could be perceived as not being that successful. However, despite the niggling injuries in my first season and the problems I had in my last season under the management of Chris Nichol, I look back on my time there fondly. The club had a strong family feel to it, and I enjoyed living and working in Southampton. I was happy playing under Lawrie McMenemy and his coaching team, and would say that the 1984–85 season in the First Division was one of the most rewarding of my career.

Like Leeds, another of my former teams, the Saints have had difficult times on and off the field in recent years, and the threat of administration hung over the club for some time. It was very sad when this came to fruition in April 2009 and the club were relegated from the Championship. They face a difficult challenge to get out of League One, especially as they will be starting with a ten-point penalty and will probably lose many of their better players.

In the summer of 1986, I realised I would be leaving the south coast, but the direction my career was to take next was extremely unexpected.

8

BLUEBIRD

I was treated well during my brief spell at the Victoria Ground with Stoke. I played quite well in my three games for the club, and I think Mick Mills, the manager, sounded out the Saints board about the possibility of a permanent transfer. But when Chris Nichol approached me about my future, I told him that I would much prefer a move back home to South Wales. In fact, I had already heard on the grapevine that the new Swansea manager Terry Yorath was keen to take me back to the Vetch.

In early July 1986, Nichol called me into his office and said, 'Curt, I think you're going to get your wish to go back home to South Wales.'

'Great! Is Terry meeting us here or in Swansea?'

There was a brief pause before Nichol continued, 'It's not Terry Yorath who's put in the offer for you, but Frank Burrows, the new Cardiff City manager.' I was taken completely by surprise.

In May 1986, both Cardiff and Swansea had been relegated from Division Three, with Frank and Terry being appointed as the new managers of the respective clubs in the same week at the end of June. I knew Frank quite well after his involvement with the youth set-up at Southampton, and I respected him, as he was a very good coach. I phoned him, and he was really enthusiastic about me joining Cardiff. During our conversation, we discussed my association with Swansea and whether he thought it would be an issue. Frank's a typical Scot, with a dry sense of humour, but he's also a straight talker, so he paused for a bit and then said, 'Curt, if you stick the blue shirt on and give 100 per cent and do the business on the park, the fans won't give two hoots who you have played for in the past.' He then reiterated how much he wanted me to sign for the club.

I have to admit that I was quite flattered by his comments and confidence in my ability to win over the Cardiff fans. However, I was still a little unsure as to the reaction I might receive at Ninian Park, so I asked Frank if he would give me 24 hours to think about it. I made a few phone calls and asked the advice of a few colleagues, including Robbie James. I respected Robbie tremendously, and my mind was made up when he basically repeated what Frank had said. He told me that genuine football fans knew their stuff and would be fully supportive of me if I was totally professional and gave my all for the shirt. He also said that if he was in my position, he would have no hesitation in signing immediately. In fact, Robbie was as good as his word, because at the very end of his career he was asked to sign for Cardiff by Eddie May and played out his career at the club.

The next day, I picked up the phone and told Frank Burrows that I was more than happy to sign for the Bluebirds on a three-year contract. If I were asked by a young player today the same question about switching between the two clubs, I would have no hesitation in offering them the same advice as Robbie offered me.

I think it's important to state that the doubts I had about signing had nothing to do with any personal issues I had with Cardiff City as a club. My only genuine concern was how I might be received by the Cardiff fans, a worry that in fact proved over time to be totally unfounded. I'm not naive enough to state that I am not aware of any rivalry that might exist between the two clubs, but for me it has never been an issue. I know that Leighton James caused some controversy with his comments that he hoped Barnsley would beat Cardiff in the semi-final of the FA Cup in 2008, but I was really pleased when they got to the final.

When I was growing up in the Rhondda in the 1960s, Cardiff attracted thousands of fans from the Valleys, many of whom would make the fortnightly train journey to Ninian Park. As a youngster, I supported all the Welsh clubs, and I still keep an eye out for the progress of all the teams, more so since I have become involved with Wales at international level. Although I wouldn't have called myself a regular by any means, I did see some good games at Ninian Park in the late 1960s and early '70s. I especially recall games against QPR with Rodney Marsh in their team and the excellent Derby County side led by Dave Mackay. Probably the most memorable game I went to as a teenager was Cardiff's famous defeat of Real Madrid in 1971. I would catch the football special from Ystrad straight into Ninian Park. However, I sometimes felt a little conspicuous going to matches, as I didn't dress in the typical football uniform for fans in the early 1970s, which consisted of a white shirt, braces, drainpipe jeans and a pair of Doc Martens boots.

I was delighted by the successes achieved by Cardiff and Swansea in 2007–08 but equally saddened that the relegation of Wrexham leaves us with only two Welsh clubs in the Football League at present. I think that perhaps supporting all the Welsh teams and wanting them to do well is a generational thing. Today, younger supporters of both teams seem to be much more partisan than when I was growing up. When I look back, I am proud that I played at international level for my country and also domestically for both the country's current league clubs.

Whenever I joined a new club, I was always determined to make a good impression, and never more so than when I turned up at Ninian Park ready to play my first season in the old Fourth Division, nearly a decade after I had last played at that level with the Swans. I signed on the dotted line for Cardiff on 7 July 1986, with managing director Ron Jones telling the local press that he believed City had been very fortunate to sign such a quality player on a free transfer. At the same press conference, Jones announced that the club had also signed a local twenty-one year old called Paul Wheeler from the Llanedeyrn area of the city on a one-year contract and that Frank Burrows would be looking to develop promising youngsters alongside more experienced players such as myself. Frank was as good as his word and made several experienced signings, including keeper Graham Moseley from Brighton and experienced pros Alan Rogers and Steve Sherlock.

Probably the biggest and definitely most controversial signing was the rugged Newport County centre-half and captain Terry Boyle. The transfer caused quite a lot of bad feeling between the clubs, which wasn't helped when the transfer tribunal priced Terry's fee at £22,000, almost half what Newport wanted for their club captain. It was evident to everybody apart from those sitting on the tribunal that Cardiff had got a bargain.

Terry proved to be a great signing for the club, as he was when he moved on to play for Swansea later in his career. He was a great leader and always gave 100 per cent commitment. I can't recall him ever missing a game because of injury, and he was a real motivating figure on the park and a real character off it. He fancied himself as something of a fashion expert and was always wearing the latest designer gear and trying to tell us that we should wear the same stuff. He was so persuasive that sometimes I think we did buy similar gear just to placate him. I'm just glad that as the 1980s was not a renowned period for fashion style, not many photographs exist of me in those Boyle-inspired get-ups!

I was determined to make a good impression at the club, and I think I certainly did when I fractured my cheekbone in the third friendly of the season. I had scored in both the previous friendlies and was feeling confident that I could continue this form into the league season. The injury made me literally speechless and down in the mouth! One side of my face had collapsed, and it was too painful for me to speak for several days. I therefore missed the first game of the new season, a scoreless draw away at Hartlepool, which saw Cardiff field six new signings.

At least I didn't miss out on the new bonus system that the club had introduced that season. We were to be paid a mouth-watering £75 per man for a league win, rising to £100 if we reached the top four after September. As the season progressed, it turned out that the club saved quite a lot of money on these bonus payments, as we only won fifteen games and never reached the giddy heights of the top four. The club also offered each player a £100 bonus if we reached at least the third round in both the League and FA cups. I'm not sure if it was a coincidence or not, but we did end up collecting these cup bonuses before being knocked out at the fourth-round stage in both competitions.

I made my league debut at Ninian Park in front of a crowd of 3,546 against Rochdale on Saturday, 30 August 1986, having made my City debut the previous Tuesday, coming on as a sub in the League Cup win at Plymouth. I was given the number 7 shirt by Frank Burrows, who told me he wanted to play me out wide in an attacking midfield role, as he believed that as I was able to hold up the ball and beat a man I could create a lot of scoring chances and make it difficult for opposition defences. Although we did create quite a few chances, we failed to convert any, and the Rochdale defence held firm. After the game, Burrows said, 'When teams come to Ninian Park, they are going to look at the good forwards we have, like Alan Curtis and Alan Rogers, and pack their goal to make things difficult for us.' I don't think Frank realised at the time he made that statement how prophetic his words would become in regards to our home performances that season.

Our next game was a tough away fixture at Molineux against title favourites Wolves, and a late Paul Wimbledon goal gave us a great victory, encouraging us to believe that we could make a real challenge for promotion. Unfortunately, for the majority of the rest of the season the curse that afflicts many football clubs struck us, namely inconsistency. Although we were capable of some excellent one-off performances, we could never string together a series of good results. After the Wolves game, we lost the next home game 2–0 to Tranmere, and up to the end of November we only won four league games, losing four and drawing a further five.

The big story coming out of the club during that period, apart from our inconsistency on the pitch, was talk in the press that we were preparing to move to an all-purpose stadium, across the park in Leckwith, by the start of the 1992 season. When confronted by the rumours, the majority of City fans were indignant, arguing that it was inconceivable that the club would move away from their Ninian Park base in their lifetime.

My own contribution to on-the-field matters was bolstered by my first goal for the club on 27 September in one of our better performances, a 4–1 hammering of Hereford. However, our contrasting form was further emphasised when we were humbled 5–1 away at Wrexham in early October. I had played in every game since the season's opener against Hartlepool, but although I felt I was generally playing well I had only found the net once and was a little concerned about my lack of goals. I think the manager realised this and called me into his office for a long chat. He said that I was working really hard, supplying good chances for others and helping to bring on the youngsters but that I needed to be far more selfish and play more for myself as well as for the team. He also reiterated that he was going to keep playing me out wide, where he thought the team would benefit most, and that I should stop worrying and just continue the job I was doing.

I was happy to work with the younger players and pass on any advice if they asked, as I had already thought seriously about coaching and had made enquiries about taking the necessary badges. During the last pre-season that Frank and I did with Cardiff, there was a suggestion that as the season developed I would perhaps lead a few training sessions, with a view to a possible coaching role in the future. However, after Frank left the club and Len Ashurst arrived, I realised that this was going to be a highly unlikely scenario under the new management set-up.

If our league form continued to fluctuate during this period, our cup performances were the opposite and showed that we were capable of some excellent football at times. In the second round of the League Cup, our opponents Luton were thrown out of the tournament after a prolonged and controversial argument about their refusal to allow away supporters to attend Kenilworth Road after rioting by Millwall fans there the previous season. Our bye to the next round gave us a plum home tie against First Division Chelsea, due to be played on 28 October, and a £10,000 cheque from the Football League as compensation for the cancellation of the Luton tie. The game proved to be a memorable one, especially for our new signing from Birmingham Nicky Platnauer, who scored both goals in the second half as we ran out 2–1 victors. Even though Chelsea were struggling near the bottom of the top flight, it was an outstanding result, as they still had big-name players such as Kerry Dixon and Pat Nevin in their side. In fact, this was one of the stand out games from my three seasons at Ninian Park. Less memorable, perhaps, was our 1–0 defeat away to Shrewsbury in the next round of the competition.

The first round of the FA Cup was also significant, although perhaps more for me personally than the team and fans, as we were drawn to face my local side Ton Pentre at Ynys Park, which was less than a mile away from my home. In fact, I could have walked to join the sell-out 2,700 crowd, as at the time I was living with my dad about five minutes' walk from the ground whilst I was waiting to sell my house in Southampton. Frank insisted that I travel to the game with the team on the coach, so I had to pass Ynys Park on my way to report for the 9 a.m. meeting at Ninian Park. In fairness to Frank, after a little bit of discussion and a little arm twisting he did say that I didn't have to travel back with the team on the pre-conditions that I played well and we won. I didn't need this extra motivation from Frank, as I was really up for the game anyway and wanted to give a good performance in front of a crowd that would contain many of my family and friends.

One of the headlines the following Monday read, 'Ton Are Toppled By Classy Curtis'. It was even more rewarding that Ton's long-serving manager Des Bartle told the press, 'Alan was Cardiff's best player. He was holding the ball up and laying it off, and if he hadn't been playing, it might have been a different story.' I was obviously pleased to have given a good account of myself, as I am especially proud of my Rhondda roots. And it was probably just as well I did have a good game, as I was frequently stopped the following week in Pentre by the locals telling me just how lucky we had been, and we exchanged some good-natured banter. God knows what it would have been like if Ton had got a result!

At the end of November, a 3–0 home victory over Cambridge United marked probably our best run of the season in the league as we won the next three games. We beat Aldershot 2–0 and Burnley 3–1, whilst also beating Bradford at home in the second round of the FA Cup, with Kevin Bartlett, our new signing from non-league football, making an instant impression with five goals in four starts. The fans were hoping that this upturn in performances would continue, starting with the Boxing Day home clash against Swansea.

I was looking forward to the Swans fixture so was a little distraught to have strained a thigh muscle in the weeks running up to the game. After all the build-up to my debut against my old club, my contribution, coming on as a sub in the 83rd minute, was hardly noticed by the crowd of 11,505, who were made to endure a dire local derby on a freezing day. In fact, it was no surprise when we were booed off by the Ninian Park faithful, who expected more from their team, especially in such an important clash between these old rivals.

What was less expected was that these jeers would be repeated at the end of every home game for the next four months, as we failed to win a home game from 13 December 1985 until 18 April 1986, a run of a dozen games. If this terrible record drove the fans to desperation, you can imagine the impact it had on Frank Burrows, who became increasingly frustrated at our inability to perform at home. In fact, our overall league form from Christmas to early May could be described as disappointing at best, as we only won a third of our 24 games.

One of the reasons for our inconsistency, I think, was that Frank was never able to find a settled formation up front. After he moved me out onto the wing, he tried an increasing number of players as striker, including loan signings Chris Pike, Dean Horrix and Tony Simmons as well as permanent signings Kevin Bartlett, Alan Rogers and Paul Wheeler. In fact, by the end of March only three teams in the division had scored fewer goals than us.

As our home form began to dip, so did the crowds at Ninian Park, and the fans started to get on the backs of the players, with a small section giving me a hard time because of my Swans connections. Although I just got on with it and didn't make any comment, I was pleased when Frank Burrows told the press that the booing I was getting was totally unwarranted and could drive me out of the club. He went on to say that I had been the outstanding player in the team during our poor run and that it would be a tragedy if I left because of this issue. Frank was very supportive and even turned down a cash offer for me from Swansea on transfer-deadline day. When he told me he had turned down their offer, I didn't really give it another thought. I believed that although I wasn't scoring regularly, I was playing well in an attacking-midfield role. I felt this was confirmed when I got a call-up for the Wales squad and was picked to play against the USSR in February in the right-midfield role that I had been fulfilling at Cardiff.

On 18 April, we finally won a game at Ninian Park for the first time in four months, beating Torquay in front of only 1,840 fans.

The game also marked my second goal of the season, and Frank Burrows told the press, somewhat tongue in cheek, that just like Ian Rush at Liverpool, every time I scored City won! After such a poor run of form, it was good to see that Frank still had a sense of humour, even if this time it was at my expense. The Torquay result was a great relief for the players, as I'm sure it was for the long-suffering City faithful.

At the end of the season, due to bad weather in January, we ended up playing our last eight games in only nineteen days. The most notable fixture in this period was my first visit to the Vetch as an opposition player. I was quite nervous about returning, but apart from the odd comment the reception I received from the Swansea fans was fine, perhaps helped by a poor Cardiff performance. At least I escaped some of the flak given to the rest of the team. The following day's *Western Mail* reported, 'Swansea outclassed a poor City side, apart from the notable exception of Alan Curtis, whose skills stood out in a laboured Cardiff performance.'

In the same week, Chris Marustik, another player who had played for both clubs, announced his retirement from the game at the age of only 25. Chris had played in the same First Division side as me at Swansea, and after my career-threatening injury at Leeds I could empathise with his difficult decision to quit the game after a persistent ankle injury.

In the last week of the season, we played four games, and in a microcosm of our season we won two, lost one and drew one. In the last home game of the season, we beat Hartlepool 4–0, a match watched by only 1,510 fans. This record lowest league attendance for the club was probably the clearest condemnation by the Cardiff fans of our performances at home that season. We finished the campaign in 13th position with 61 points, having won 15 games, drawn 16 and lost 15. To the great chagrin of the Cardiff fans, we also finished one place below Swansea and four places below Wrexham in the league table.

Even though as a team our season was quite indifferent, I felt that I had played pretty consistently, appearing in over 50 league and cup games. The two issues that had caused me some concern during the season had been my lack of goals, as I ended up with only four, and the negative reaction I had received from a very small section of the crowd during our terrible midseason home run. I had worked very hard in an unaccustomed role on the right flank in an attempt to repay Frank Burrows' faith in me and win over the Cardiff fans. So you can imagine how thrilled I was when it was announced that I had won the vote as the supporters' Player of the Year.

Over the summer, Frank sold Mel Rees to Watford for £100,000 and used some of the money to strengthen the squad. Probably his best signing was the former England youth international Jimmy Gilligan, a bargain at just £17,500 from Lincoln City. We also signed Brian McDermott and Phil Bater, and Nigel Stevenson, another ex-Swansea colleague, joined us from the Vetch on a free. We thought that with the squad we had we could make a real challenge for promotion, but we realised that we would have to perform much better at home than the previous season. The 1987–88 season also saw all four Welsh clubs not only in the bottom tier of the Football League for the first time ever, but in the same division for the first time also.

Our season started indifferently and initially seemed to suggest to the fans that they were going to witness more of the same as the previous year. A home draw against Leyton Orient was followed by an away defeat at Bolton, and we also failed to beat Newport in either leg of our League Cup tie. We lost 4–3 on aggregate despite the fact that we played both legs at home after Newport's summer cash crisis meant they had yet to segregate Somerton Park in order to be able to cater for away fans.

After such a poor start to the season, the next home game would be crucial, especially as it was against Swansea, who had also started their campaign badly. In fact, it was our best performance for a long time, and although we only won 1–0, through a Jimmy Gilligan goal, we really could have scored three or four. This win gave us the boost we needed and marked a run of form that saw us lose only one of the next nine games, winning six and drawing a further two. Our only defeat was at Wrexham, which I realised was going to be a long day when I missed the players' bus and had to travel up with the supporters club in their coach. Before they would let me get on the bus, they made me join the club, and I had to pay £5, which was the annual subscription rate at the time.

The day didn't look any more promising when it was announced that Joey Jones had overcome a niggling injury and was passed fit to play. You always knew you were going to have a tough afternoon when Joey was marking you. I had played in the same Wales youth team with Joey, and at all subsequent levels, so we knew each other's games and got on really well. Joey was what we used to call an uncompromising defender – hard but fair. Like many tough defenders of that era, it is debatable as to whether he would have survived in the current Premier League, where yellow cards are handed out like confetti at times. I'm sure that he would have adapted, as he played at the highest level with Wales and Liverpool, with whom he won the European Cup. In Continental football in the 1970s, there were many clever attacking players who could win a free-kick or get a defender booked, sometimes seemingly out of thin air, and subsequently defenders had to be very wary of whistle-happy foreign referees. In my view, domestic football, especially at the highest level, has become more like Continental football was back then, and good players such as Joey would always be able to adapt to changing patterns and styles of play.

During this derby game, it wasn't Joey who went in the referee's notebook but Phil Bater, who became the first City player ever to be sent off on his debut, making a 3–0 defeat inevitable. It had been an interesting day but one I filed under 'hopefully not to be repeated again'.

In contrast to the previous season, our home form was excellent, and we didn't lose our first match at Ninian Park until 10 October against Hereford. We only lost one other match at home all season. My memories of the Hereford game are still vivid, and not just because we lost our unbeaten home record and suffered the first defeat at Ninian Park in 15 games. The game marked my first sending off in 472 league games and was only the second time I had received my marching orders. I'm in no way condoning players taking the law into their own hands, but sometimes even the calmest players can see the 'red mist', and this was one such occasion for me.

I felt the Hereford players had targeted me for special treatment from the start of the game. Close to half-time, I was fouled for the umpteenth time, and as I got up their stalwart defender Mel Pejic made a comment. We both engaged in some pushing and shoving and got booked. Shortly after the break, I was running down the wing and their full-back Steve Devine nearly cut me in half with a tackle. The next time he got the ball, I followed through with my challenge, and the referee Tony Ward gave me a second yellow. Although he probably had little choice but to send me off, I felt that if he had cracked down on their challenges much earlier in the game, I would probably not have retaliated the way I did. This was one of the problems of being seen as a creative player in the Fourth Division. Unless you had a strong ref, opposition defenders had a free licence to use you for target practice, especially away from home.

I felt completely gutted that I had let the side down and made a public apology to the manager and players. The fact that we lost the game to a controversial penalty didn't improve my mood one bit. The thirteenth league game of the season had proved to be especially unlucky for me, as I also received a two-match suspension from the Welsh FA.

In the run up to Christmas, we remained in the top six, and defeats in the first round of the FA Cup and Associate Members Cup meant we could, as the well-worn cliché goes, concentrate on the league.

On 29 December, we travelled to Colchester. If we had won, we would have replaced them at the top of the table, but a 2–1 defeat meant we started the new year three points behind the team from Essex, competing for the promotion places with Wolves, Orient and Bolton.

The winter months of January and February are probably the most difficult for a professional footballer. It can be a hard slog playing through the terrible weather, especially on the poor pitches of the lower divisions. It's also a period when teams tend to consolidate their challenge for honours or confirm themselves as relegation candidates. As a team, we were very focused on ensuring that we would still be on the hunt for promotion when the season came to a close. And there was no better demonstration of our team spirit than when we scored twice in the last six minutes to secure a creditable draw at the Vetch on New Year's Day 1988.

At the end of January, a 4–0 victory over Cambridge United put us in an automatic promotion place and also marked the debut of a great character, the former Everton and Scotland goalie George Wood. In fact, George became one of six different keepers we used that season because of injuries. George had come to the club with a reputation as being a bit awkward and grumpy, but at Cardiff he was a great teammate, good fun to be with and also an excellent and very brave keeper. In fact, he was still turning out and keeping clean sheets in the League of Wales well into his late 40s, as well as coaching at Ninian Park. Very recently I came across his son James, who was playing against Wales for Scotland Under-17s, even though he could have also played for us, as he was actually born in Wales. I'm sure George, who was a former Scottish international himself and very proud of his roots, would have had a little word to push him in the right direction, and I'll keep an eye out for the progress of Wood junior.

The month of February would be crucial for our fortunes, as we were due to face three of our closest challengers for promotion:

Wolves, Colchester and Leyton Orient. These games saw us give both our best and worst away performances of the season, a 4–1 defeat of Wolves at Molineux matched by a woeful defeat by Orient by the same score two weeks later. After the Brisbane Road debacle, Frank Burrows laid down the law in no uncertain terms, reminding us that if we thought we were already promoted, we were in for a rude awakening and that we had to treat every game as if it were a cup final, just as the other promotion candidates certainly would.

The 'hairdryer treatment' from Frank must have worked a treat, as in the last three months of the season we only lost twice, and there were no repeats of the Orient performance. Although we were confident about our chances, by mid-March only six points separated the next ten teams behind leaders Wolves, so we knew we couldn't afford any slip-ups.

A 2–0 victory away at Exeter marked the beginning of a remarkable run-in to the end of the season, when we won seven of the next eight games and allayed any nerves the fans might have felt. And we finished the season in some style, winning our last five games of what had turned out to be a great season for the club. On 23 April, we beat Scarborough in front of 5,751 fans, a game that marked only my first league goal of the season. Whenever I meet Cardiff supporters, they always remind me that even though I only scored a few goals for the Bluebirds they always seemed to be quite spectacular efforts. I remember this goal in particular, which came from a free-kick, because as I bent it around the wall I couldn't see where it had gone and only knew I'd scored when I heard the roar from the fans behind the goal in the Grange End. In fact, I think after that the next four or five goals I scored for the club all came from free-kicks outside the box.

After a scrappy 1–0 away victory at Hartlepool, we faced Crewe at home, knowing that a point would be enough for us to gain automatic promotion. We went into the game on seventy-nine points, having played forty-four games, six points ahead of Scunthorpe, who were in fourth place, having played the same number of matches as us. On a muggy bank holiday Monday evening, over ten thousand fans celebrated as we eased past Crewe by two goals to secure promotion. It was a fantastic evening, and as we celebrated long into the night I felt a real sense of achievement. I think Frank Burrows should take a lot of credit for our success, as he had built a promotion side on a tight budget, having spent only £40,000 on players in his first two seasons at the club.

On the last day of the season, we faced Burnley at Turf Moor, which marked another special occasion in a fantastic season, as I reached my 500th league appearance. I marked the game with my second goal of the campaign from another free-kick. I was not quite as prolific as Jimmy Gilligan, who scored his 20th in a 2–1 win, and he deservedly won the Player of the Year plaudits.

We had finished the season in style as runners-up to Wolves, and several weeks later we were followed into Division Three by Swansea, who won promotion through the newly introduced play-off system. One sad footnote was that Newport County, who had struggled against financial meltdown all season, were relegated from the Football League and went bankrupt before the end of their first season in the Conference before being reformed as Newport AFC.

Two weeks after gaining promotion, we were to face Wrexham in the final of the Welsh Cup, with qualification for the Cup-Winners' Cup still on the table at that time. With Cardiff reaching the final of the FA Cup in 2008, the whole issue of Welsh clubs playing in England and qualifying for European competition became something of a hot potato once again. I understand the reasoning behind the Welsh FA barring the teams playing in the English pyramid from competing in the Welsh Cup as of 1995, but the tournament has certainly lost a lot of its appeal. With no disrespect intended to our non-league clubs, the Welsh clubs' record in Europe since then has been very disappointing, and I think the cup does miss the teams playing in England. It could also be argued that if the Welsh clubs based in the English pyramid could offer European football as well as Championship football, they would probably be able to attract a far better quality of player to the Liberty or Ninian Park.

Back in 1988, we began our Welsh Cup campaign in inauspicious circumstances, drawing at home with Ebbw Vale before beating them in a replay. The competition then saw us overcome Port Talbot, Merthyr and Caernarfon before facing our Division Four rivals in the final at the Vetch Field. It was probably a good thing for some of the lads that the game was played nearly a fortnight after our promotion celebrations! Surprisingly for a club who had won the Welsh Cup 20 times, City hadn't qualified for Europe for 12 years, so we had every incentive to cap off a great season in style in front of a large crowd made up of mostly Cardiff fans.

Players enjoy playing in and can recall cup-final appearances at whatever level they play, but for me the 1988 Welsh Cup final was especially unforgettable, as I scored one of my best ever goals. I know that the goal against Leeds for the Swans is probably my most famous one, the one I scored for Leeds at the Dell extremely memorable and my strike for Southampton against Arsenal one to be proud of, but I think that the one for Cardiff in the cup final was probably my best ever. I watched it again recently, and it still feels as though everything happened in slow motion.

Midway through the first half, I received the ball from a throw-in on the halfway line. With my back to goal and two Wrexham players behind me, I dragged the ball back, spun around and managed to pass between both of them before beating another couple of defenders on a 30-yard run that took me towards the corner flag and the edge of their box. I looked up with every intention of crossing the ball, but there were no City players attacking, so I cut back inside. As I ran across the edge of the box, three red-shirted defenders converged on me, so I just decided to have a go with my left peg, and I was delighted when my 25-yard shot curled into the corner of Mike Salmon's goal. As I ran off to celebrate, I heard Nicky Platnauer shout out to another

City player, 'I didn't think Curt could run so fast.' The goal and the fact that it helped the club qualify for Europe for the first time in over a decade capped a great season.

The 1988–89 season promised much for the long-suffering Cardiff fans, and Tony Clemo, the club chairman, assured Frank Burrows that funds would be made available so that we could challenge for another promotion. However, the anticipation of the close season turned into anxiety as the new campaign got underway and both players and fans realised that money for new personnel had not materialised. Despite the club receiving a record £150,000 from Oxford for midfielder Mike Ford, our only signings were the £35,000 paid to Hereford for full-back Ian Rodgerson and the signings of Steve Tupling and Steve Lynex on frees.

The first game of 1988–89 saw us lose 2–1 at home to Fulham, and in a poor start we only won one league fixture during the first three months of the season, including a 6–1 reverse at Port Vale, the club's worst defeat in over a decade. The only positive note for the fans came in the cup competitions, as we overcame a 1–0 home-leg defeat at Swansea in the League Cup. Our 2–0 victory at the Vetch was Cardiff's first win there for 30 years. In the Cup-Winners' Cup, the promise of a financially beneficial European run was increased by a first-round victory over Derry City before a disappointing 6–1 aggregate defeat to the Danish cup holders Aarhus.

As we faced Bury at home on 1 November, the alarm bells were beginning to ring, as we were third from bottom of the table with seven points, the same number as bottom club Chesterfield. However, the Bury game sparked a major improvement in performances, and we seemed to be turning the corner, as victory over the Lancashire club was followed by three consecutive 1–0 home victories over Gillingham, Northampton and Brentford. Our seven-match winning streak also saw us beat Hereford and Enfield in the FA Cup and knock Swansea out of the Sherpa Van Trophy, now the Johnstone's Paint Trophy. In fairness, this run corresponded with the only time that Frank Burrows had a full squad to call upon in what turned out to be an injury-ravaged season for the club.

By Christmas, our form had again dipped, and a further bout of injuries only served to dent the team's confidence as we were knocked out of both cup competitions. Our league form also began to suffer, and after I had scored a late winner at Aldershot in early January we only managed to win eight of the final twenty-seven league games. And the injury jinx that had plagued the club all season affected me personally against Bolton in January when a badly bruised rib kept me out for six games.

The team's performances were not helped in the first few months of 1989 by the constant rumours that Frank Burrows and strikers Jimmy Gilligan and Kevin Bartlett were all on their way out of the club. After an embarrassing 3–1 Welsh Cup defeat at Kidderminster, the prospect of no European football and the closing of that avenue of finance seemed to accelerate the move of Kevin to West Brom for £100,000. Although Tony Clemo argued this marked a great profit for the club, he reiterated that none of the money from Kevin's sale would be available to the manager to sign a replacement. This gave the clear impression to the players and the fans that Cardiff lacked ambition and was now a 'selling' club. This was backed up by the evidence, as in his first two and a half years at the club Frank had only spent £85,000 on players whilst recouping nearly £400,000 in sales.

Nearly 20 years later, I can see some similar parallels with what has happened to Dave Jones, the current Cardiff manager. Jones has been forced to sell many of his talented players during his tenure, including Chris Gunter and Aaron Ramsey, and therefore did a fabulous job to subsequently assemble a team to reach the 2008 FA Cup final with little or no funds. I had a sense of déjà vu after the final when rumours abounded that a Cardiff cash crisis meant they would be forced to listen to offers for their most talented young players. Teams who continually sell their best youngsters can give a negative message to potential signings and the clubs' own quality players when they are deciding whether or not they should renew their contracts, and consequently they can never quite push on to the next level so often talked about by managers and fans alike.

Back in 1989, the off-field saga continued as the resignation of director Gerald McCarthy over his opposition to the sale of Bartlett to West Brom dominated the back pages. In February, Tony Clemo then announced that he was selling the club, allegedly due to his unwillingness to fund ground improvements and City's continued reputation for hooliganism.

The failure to buy a replacement for Bartlett, who had scored 13 goals so far that season, seemed to put even more pressure on Jimmy Gilligan, who now struggled to hit the net having scored freely for 18 months. By late March, we were only seven points off the relegation places, and despite a run of four unbeaten games in April we still entered the last few weeks of the season looking over our shoulders at the form of the teams below us. On bank holiday Monday, in an atmosphere that was in stark contrast to the party mood of the same day the previous year, an immediate return to the bottom division became a real possibility as we lost at home to Chesterfield, who were at that time occupying the last relegation place. This meant that we were only three points ahead of them with four games to go. After a team meeting and some home truths from Frank Burrows, we managed to conjure up one last effort, and three draws and a victory meant we managed to stave off relegation as we limped to the end of a hugely disappointing season for all concerned with the club.

We had eventually finished the season in 16th place, and the injury crisis that had dominated the season only served to highlight the failure to invest in the squad that season. The decision not to buy a replacement for Kevin Bartlett was also reflected in the figures, as we scored only 44 goals in 46 league games.

As my third season with the club came to an end, so did my contract, and I was really unsure as to where my future lay. There was still a lot of confusion surrounding the fact that the club remained up for sale, and Frank Burrows had yet to sign a new deal. I felt that even at the age of 35 I still had at least another year to offer at that level, and I had played 44 league and cup games that season so didn't think my fitness was an issue.

With the turmoil off the pitch, the club seemed to realise that money would be tight for whoever owned Cardiff City at the start of the new season and that any new signings would be unlikely. Therefore, in order to impart some sense of stability, eleven players, including me, were offered new one-year deals. I was happy to sign, and at that time I fully believed that I would be playing at least another full season for the Bluebirds, possibly even another one after that.

During the close season, the exodus of key players continued as Paul Wimbledon was sold for £60,000, Nicky Platnauer joined Notts County for £50,000 and Terry Boyle was sold to Swansea for £24,000. Whilst these key players left, Frank Burrows only made two signings: full-back Ray Daniel from Hull for £40,000 and Cardiff-born Chris Pike joined on a free from Fulham.

When the season kicked off against Bolton, Frank announced that I was to be his club captain. This was a great honour, but I also worried it could be a bit of a poisoned chalice, as I thought we might struggle to stay in the division with the squad we had. Our lack of experience was highlighted by the fact that in the 2–0 defeat by Bolton in the first game of the season the team contained seven players aged twenty-two or under.

After only a week of the new season, Frank dropped the bombshell that he was leaving the club to become John Gregory's assistant at Portsmouth. I had worked with Frank off and on for nearly five years, and we'd developed a very good relationship. I think he proved himself to be an excellent manager, especially in the lower leagues, where he must have been a chairman's dream. He had the knack of getting players on free transfers or from non-league clubs and then selling them on for large profits, and he did this at Cardiff and later during his successful four years with Swansea.

Some of the most vivid memories I have of Frank are his contributions to five-a-side games during training sessions at Cardiff. He was in his 40s at the time and still thought he could show us a thing or two about how the game should be played. His version was competitive to say the least, and you prayed that you were on his side, as he never shirked a challenge, even if it was the day before the next league game. Some people might argue that he perhaps never really fulfilled his potential as a manager, but I enjoyed every minute as a player under him and thought he was both a thoughtful and inspiring coach.

Within a week, the club had announced that Len Ashurst would be joining the club as manager for a second time. You never really know where you are with a new boss, but initially there seemed to be no problem when Ashurst named me captain for his first game in charge, a 2–2 draw at home to Brentford. As club skipper, I made every effort to motivate the players, but the lack of experience and quality in the squad was becoming more evident, and by the end of September we were rooted to the bottom of the table, with only two points from eight games. Our predicament didn't improve when our top scorer for the past two seasons, Jimmy Gilligan, followed our ex-manager to Portsmouth for a then club record fee of £215,000.

Early the following week, after a 4–0 defeat to Rotherham, Len Ashurst called me to his office and announced, somewhat to my surprise, that I didn't figure in his plans for the future of the club. He also said that Swansea were interested in signing me and that I could go for a nominal fee. I think Ashurst was trying to reshape things and put his own much firmer stamp on the club. Training had become far more regimented and was twice as long as it had been previously but didn't really seem to achieve much apart from putting more pressure on the players both mentally and physically.

When he announced his intentions, I had mixed emotions. After being skipper for the first ten games of the season, I didn't want the fans to think I was deserting a sinking ship. On the other hand, the manager had made it very clear that I had no future at Ninian Park.

Although I would be sad to leave Cardiff I was also hugely excited about the opportunity that I was being offered, as I'd always thought that I'd like to finish my career with Swansea.

I thoroughly enjoyed my time with the Bluebirds, and in my 150 appearances for the club I'd like to think that I always gave my best effort in every game in the Blue shirt and hope that the Ninian Park fans feel the same. However, I also think that the club was very badly run by the board, and they seemed to have no ambition. Their unwillingness to allow Frank Burrows to sign any new players after our excellent promotion season of 1987–88 was short-sighted to say the least. It was somewhat inevitable that the club were relegated at the end of the 1989–90 season, and I believe that the fans and players deserved better treatment from the board than they were given.

After the initial disappointment of my meeting with Ashurst, I became very positive about the opportunity being offered to me to end my career where it had all started. The conclusion of my playing career was now going to be written in the same place as the first chapter, 17 years after I had first travelled there as a teenager from Pentre in 1972.

9

SWANSONG

On 4 October 1989, I rejoined the Swans for my third spell with the team. At that time, they were sitting in twenty-second place in a league of twenty-four, having only gained five points from seven games. But my motivation for returning to the club was simple. Like many players coming to the end of their playing days, I wanted to play out my career at the club I felt was my 'home'.

Although many professionals cite a desire to see out their last few seasons at their favourite club, it doesn't always work out that way. John Hartson is a case in point. He made no secret of his desire to finish at his home-town club, but unfortunately, due to issues concerning his fitness, it never happened for him, and I think he was very disappointed he didn't get a chance to pull on the white shirt of Swansea. Therefore, I am very grateful that I was able to see out my last season at my chosen club.

As I walked through the players' entrance at the Vetch for the first time in six years, I could have been stepping straight back into the past, as the club, much like when I left, was in turmoil on and off the field. Although the position the club found itself in was certainly no laughing matter, I did manage a wry smile to myself, as we had also been struggling to avoid relegation from Division Three when I joined the club back in 1972 – a definite case of déjà vu.

Just before I arrived, there were more problems for the club off the field when trouble flared during the first leg of the Cup-Winners' Cup tie in Greece against Panathinaikos and ten Swans fans were jailed by the Greek authorities. The Greek club appealed to UEFA for the return game to be played on the Continent, claiming that they feared reprisals against their players and fans, although their narrow 3–2 victory might have also played a part in them wanting to avoid a potentially volatile second leg in Wales. The appeal was dismissed, but the second leg was unfortunately drawn 3–3, so my chance to sample more European competition had evaporated before I'd even arrived.

I was signed by my ex-Wales colleague Ian Evans, but even as I put pen to paper the local press was rife with rumours that the manager's position was in jeopardy, especially as the team had suffered a 6–1 home reverse to Reading in the week leading up to my transfer. One local paper even suggested that I was his last throw of the dice in a desperate gamble to win back the support of the fans – so no pressure on me, then! I had come back to help the club out, play when I was needed and bring on some of the promising youngsters, and as somebody who had always tried to shun press coverage I have to say that the fuss did make me feel more than a little uncomfortable.

The perceived cloud over the team was not helped when chairman Doug Sharpe put the club up for sale, just as Tony Clemo had at Cardiff the previous season. I think both Sharpe and Clemo as successful local businessmen took over the chairmanship of their respective clubs with the best of intentions to help out. However, they were perhaps a little naive when it came to running a football club and understanding just how much of their money would be needed to maintain success. After ploughing a lot of their own cash into the teams, both chairmen realised that running a football club could sometimes seem like a licence to burn money. Both chairmen therefore called for a more businesslike approach to running the finances of the clubs, which inevitably put them into conflict with the fans, who having been promised a new dawn were seemingly once again left with a familiar tale of empty promises and sales of their favourite players.

Despite the Swans' struggles in the league, there was still the nucleus of a good squad. Roger Freestone, a popular keeper, was on loan from Chelsea, having lost his place there to Dave Beasant. Roger was supported in defence by future Wales internationals Chris Coleman and Andy Melville, as well as former Wales centre-half Terry Boyle. Chris was quite naive in those days, and I remember one incident against Merthyr in the Welsh Cup that season in particular. We were losing, and the crowd was getting on the players' backs, especially Chris, who responded by giving some of our fans the two fingers. Needless to say, he regretted it after the game and had to apologise. It was an experience that as a successful manager he probably uses to advise any youngster who finds himself in a similar situation: don't respond to the crowd whatever the provocation.

Chris went on to have a great career at both club and international level before a very serious car crash prematurely ended his playing days. I got on well with him and watched his managerial career with interest. I was very grateful to him when he was manager of Fulham and brought the club down to the Liberty to play in my testimonial in 2005.

We also had the experience of Robbie James and Tommy Hutchison in midfield, and John Salako was impressing on loan from Crystal Palace. Promising youngster Andy Legg, who later moved to Cardiff, where his long throw and wholehearted efforts made him a cult favourite at Ninian Park and helped him win six Wales caps, was also in the squad.

My first match – I can't really call it my debut – came against Crewe at the Vetch the following Saturday. It was a very surreal situation, as although I had already played 348 league games for the club I was really nervous. Despite not normally being the worrying type, I didn't sleep a wink the night before and was up and out of the house early, going for a long walk to try and clear my head. I didn't want the other players or the Swansea fans to think that I was rejoining the club on some sort of personal nostalgia trip, and I was as eager to perform well as I had been when I played my first game in 1972. I really wanted to help the club to get out of the trough it found itself in.

Despite my initial nerves, I enjoyed the game, which turned out to be a cracker. We won 3–2, and I was happy to have played a part in all three of our goals. However, I also knew that Crewe were far from the strongest team in the division, and we would have a long way to go before we could feel safe.

I was fortunate that my rejoining the club coincided with a much improved run of form, as we won five and drew one of the next eight games. My worries that I might struggle to contribute to the team were eased, as I scored the winning goals in 1–0 victories over Bury, Tranmere and Rotherham during that spell. This certainly helped dispel any lingering doubts I might have had about my decision to transfer back to the Vetch and convinced me that I had made the right decision.

By early November, we were in the top ten, and I hoped that I had repaid the manager's faith in re-signing me and the support I had received from the Vetch faithful. Ian Evans' position also seemed much more secure, as he was allowed to spend over a quarter of a million on striker Paul Chalmers and defender Keith Walker from St Mirren, as well as John Hughes from Berwick. Chalmers had a great pedigree, as he was the son of former Celtic striker Steve, one of the legendary Lisbon Lions who beat Inter Milan in the 1967 European Cup final. Unfortunately, Paul and John struggled to settle at the Vetch and both returned to play in the Scottish leagues. Keith, or 'Sky' as he was nicknamed, settled far more quickly in South Wales and was a great servant to the Swans throughout the 1990s, representing the club in over 300 games.

I'm not sure why, but in recent years the stream of talent from Scotland into the English leagues seems to have dried up. In the 1970s and '80s, all the best teams – Leeds, Liverpool, Manchester United – had a core of three or four quality Scots, and the Scottish international team was a real force in European football. Maybe it has something to do with the increasing availability of relatively less-expensive foreign players these days.

Despite the relative improvement on the field, off the pitch the club was still running its affairs in the manner of a very bad soap opera. I know some people believe that off-the-field incidents should not affect professional footballers, but there were a lot of youngsters in the squad, and all the in-fighting was bound to have an impact. Harry Hyde, who was a director of our sponsors DP, the fitness products company, had resigned as a company director, so the Swans took legal action to remove him from the football board. Harry would not go, and it was highly embarrassing at post-match social events, because the man who replaced him at DP was also there. Additionally, the future of the club's ownership was still shrouded in doubt, as Doug was trying to sell the club to a London businessman. Robbie and I had seen all this before, but the kids did not know if they would be at the club from one week to the next.

As we entered the new decade, our form dipped, but we were still 12th in the table, and the early season worries over a relegation fight had seemingly disappeared. What I particularly remember about that period was the growing excitement that had developed around the club as a result of us being paired with First Division leaders Liverpool at home in the third round of the FA Cup. Swansea versus Liverpool had been a First Division fixture only seven seasons previously, when only twelve league positions had separated the teams. In January 1990, 58 league places marked the difference between the teams, as well as an equally huge gulf in resources and quality. I would like to say we were unlucky not to pull off a shock victory as the famous 1964 team had done in that season's quarter-final against the same club. In fairness, though, the Reds dominated the match, and we were relatively happy to get a goalless draw, thanks mainly to our goalkeeper Lee Bracey, who'd returned to the team because Chelsea had recalled Roger Freestone from his loan period. Lee had had a torrid time earlier in the season when the crowd had really got on his back, and his loss of confidence had directly led to Roger's loan spell at the club. It was good, therefore, to see him play so well and silence some of his more vociferous critics.

I really enjoyed the game and felt our efforts in achieving a replay against a star-studded Liverpool side were appreciated by the Vetch fans. (I know the chairman was also happy at the extra cash a replay at Anfield would bring.) The Liverpool team that day was Bruce Grobbelaar, Glenn Hysén, Barry Venison, Steve Nicol, Ronnie Whelan, Alan Hansen, Peter Beardsley, Steve Staunton, Ian Rush, John Barnes and Steve McMahon, and they went on to win their 18th league title that season. I remember coming off the field absolutely shattered and joking with Ian Rush that he never looked like scoring. Ian is a lovely guy, and despite being one of the best strikers Britain has ever seen he just smiled and said, 'We'll see you back at Anfield, Curt.'

The replay took place the following Tuesday, and we were confident that we could put up a good performance and perhaps even pull off a shock. We couldn't have been more mistaken, as we were on the wrong side of an eight-goal hiding. I think our keeper Lee Bracey must have been shell-shocked, as three days earlier he had kept a clean sheet, and he must have been fully aware of the old cliché, 'You're only as good as your last game.' As for Rushie, well, of course, he scored a hat-trick, but being the guy he is he never mentioned it.

The Liverpool tie had really built up excitement amongst the players and the fans, and I think the nature of the defeat at Anfield knocked the confidence out of the team. Our league form disintegrated, and we only won three of our next sixteen games. When results dip, the manager's position inevitably comes under intense scrutiny, and by the middle of March Ian Evans was sacked after less than a year at the Vetch. To everybody's great surprise, Terry Yorath returned to the club as manager after only 13 months away. Terry had been a popular manager at the Vetch, but his relationship with the fans and especially the chairman Doug Sharpe had been severely strained when he had broken his contract and left for Bradford. In fact, the Swans were still in dispute with the Yorkshire club over compensation payments.

Not only was Terry under pressure to turn around fortunes at the Vetch, but he was also part-time manager of Wales, who were suffering from a poor World Cup qualifying campaign, having failed to win any of their six games. I think that by this stage international football management was a full-time job, and Terry was always going to be up against it trying to combine the two posts. I thought that Terry would be one of the last to combine club and national management at the same time, so Guus Hiddink taking over Chelsea in February 2009 whilst still managing the Russian national team was a major surprise and inevitably opened him up to much criticism, especially in Russia.

Terry's return to the club didn't spark the desired improvement in our fortunes that everybody wished for, and his first game at the Vetch saw us crash 5–0 to Bristol City. Things didn't get much better, as we also lost the next three games without getting on the score sheet, and only 2,582 fans watched the home defeat to Leyton Orient. As we entered the Easter weekend, our status as a Third Division club was still precarious, and an Easter Monday fixture at Ninian Park promised to be even more competitive than normal, as Cardiff, who occupied the last relegation place, had 43 points compared to our total of 46.

Before the derby match, I told the chairman and the manager that I would be retiring at the end of the season. I didn't make the decision lightly, and when I had come back to the club it had been my intention to hopefully play on until the end of the 1990–91 season. However, as the campaign had progressed, I had increasingly picked up niggling

injuries and was finding it harder to play two or three games a week
and train every day. It was the training that was really the issue, as
despite the fact that I had always kept myself very fit I realised that
as I entered my 36th year I needed to give my body more time to
recover. I had a great relationship with Frank Burrows at Cardiff, and
we had a good understanding that if I was struggling after a match
and missed the odd training session, it wasn't an issue. However, both
Ian Evans and Terry Yorath were under great pressure to turn around
a struggling side and probably felt if they had allowed me to miss the
odd day from training, it might give the wrong message to the rest of
the squad. I felt I could continue for another season, but I wouldn't
be able to play in every game and train all week, and I wasn't prepared
to compromise by giving anything less than 100 per cent, so I realised
that after 20 years my time as a professional had come to its natural
conclusion.

As the crucial Ninian Park fixture approached, I wondered if Terry
would continue to pick me in the first team after my announcement,
so I was determined to play well when he told me that I was in the
starting XI against Cardiff. I had no desire for my career to be played
out in a side that was relegated.

The derby match was a particularly dire one and probably
demonstrated why both clubs were struggling at the bottom of the
league. Crucially, though, we won the game 2–0, and these vital
points meant that the gap between ourselves and Blackpool, who
now occupied the last relegation place, was five points. A 3–0 win
over Wigan in our next game widened the gap between us and the
Bloomfield Road club to seven points and seemed to make our
position all but safe. However, at the end of a season those teams at
the bottom of the league who are fighting for their lives all typically
begin to win, and it was the same in 1990. In our next two games,
we failed to get the win we needed, drawing a vital game against
Blackpool 2–2 and losing 3–0 to Preston on their plastic pitch.

I had hoped that my last game as a Swans player would be a

relaxed affair, perhaps with a typical end-of-season holiday feel about it. Instead, the game was a crucial one, not only for us, but also for our opponents Bolton, who were pushing for promotion, and neither team could afford to lose the game. With so much at stake, I knew Terry wouldn't give in to sentiment and that my selection wasn't automatic. So, I was hugely relieved when he named the team and I was in. He said that he needed all my experience to help the team through the game.

Although I was pleased to get the selection nod, my mind started to race, and on the Friday before the match I began to think how terrible it would be if we were relegated in my last game and what an anticlimax it would be. On the Saturday morning, I took a walk along the Mumbles before breakfast. Suddenly, I began to feel much more positive. Any nerves seemed to wash away with the early morning tide, and I began to look forward to the match.

I'd like to say that my last game for the club, which was witnessed by 5,000 fans, was a memorable one and that we played football equal to the quality of that famous win over Leeds in 1981. Unfortunately, the only similarity between the two days was the scorching sun that warmed the short-sleeved fans on the terraces. By half-time, both sides seemed to have come to the conclusion that a point each would be a good result. At the end of the game, there was a pitch invasion, and for a few seconds I was a little nervous, as a large section of the crowd started to head in my direction. However, my worries quickly proved unfounded as I was hoisted on the shoulders of several fans and chaired off the field in a party-like atmosphere. I was by that stage more worried for the lads who were carrying me, as I had certainly put on a few pounds since my debut for the club 18 years before.

My last game for the Swans also marked the end for the Double Decker, which, much like me, seemed to be on its last legs. The famous old stand was to be demolished as part of the upgrading of football stadiums insisted on by the Taylor Report, which was set up after the Hillsborough disaster.

During the last few minutes of the Bolton game, I started to feel quite emotional and had a lump in my throat as memories of my career came flooding back. I pictured Roy Bentley with his arm around me before my debut at Southend in 1972, telling me to go out and enjoy myself. I recalled the dressing-room after another heavy defeat in the mid-1970s, Harry Gregg letting off steam and the air blue with industrial language as he told us we were all useless so-and-sos. I remembered Tosh's words that summer afternoon in 1981 as we faced Leeds and he told me to go out and prove to all those critics who said I couldn't hack it at the top level just how wrong they were. Above all, I remembered my mentor and friend Harry Griffiths. I could picture him saying, 'Well done, son! Well done!'

I was very grateful for the reception the fans gave me and was delighted to be finishing my career with the Swans and playing my last game at the Vetch. However, I thought that apart from watching the team as a fan, my association with the club had come to an end.

Although I had a few potential offers to continue with another league club, the following season I had no intention of carrying on as a full-time pro. So I was very interested when the Barry Town chairman David Sylvester contacted me and offered me the chance to go and play for them. Barry were at that time a part-time club in the Beazer Homes Midland Division. They had a distinguished record, having played for over sixty years in the old Southern League before returning to the Welsh pyramid in 1982, where they subsequently won six of the next seven league titles. However, at the start of the 1990–91 season, the club had decided to return to the English league system, and David and manager Andy Beattie felt that my experience would be invaluable in helping some of the youngsters breach the gap in standards.

When I arrived at the club, there was no discussion over terms. David just asked me what size shirt and trousers I wore and told me to come back and have a chat with Andy later in the week. When I returned, a brand new blazer and slacks were waiting for me, and Andy was great and made me feel really wanted by the club.

I really enjoyed the season in the Southern League, and the standard of football was very good. Most of the clubs had ex-pros, and amongst others we played against Mark Lawrenson with Corby Town and ex-Forest star John Robertson with Grantham. Training with Andy was a lot of fun, and we played a lot of five-a-side. I seemed to practise penalties and free-kicks a lot. I think he knew that quite a few of us were very experienced players who didn't need to be run into the ground in training and would be better saving our legs for the matches themselves. In fact, I think that most of the squad had at least some league experience, and players such as Paul Wimbledon, David Hough, Terry Boyle and ex-Birmingham and Norwich star Keith Bertschin had hundreds of league games under their belts.

However, there was a lot of travelling, and after some midweek games I wouldn't get back home to Swansea much before three or four in the morning. This was pretty hard, as I was working full-time as well. So, at the end of the season I reluctantly informed David and Andy that I wouldn't be playing the following season.

I still wanted to play regularly, so when I got an offer from Ray Davies at Haverfordwest in the Welsh League I was happy to join them. Ray, who has sadly passed away now, was a great bloke. Despite the fact that the club was based 45 miles away, the majority of the players were from the Swansea area, so we trained twice a week in the city, and on Saturdays Ray would pick us up in his old minibus and take us to the games.

Near the end of that season, I was also asked to help out at Caerau FC, the team my dad had played for. I played a few games for them, including the last of the season, which we won 2–0 against Skewen to win promotion, and I managed to bag both goals. My dad was at the match, and I never saw him so happy about a game I played in.

I remember him telling me that in playing for Caerau he felt I had finally reached the pinnacle of my footballing career.

After an enjoyable season with Haverfordwest, I was asked by Morriston to join them for the start of the 1992–93 season. Although it was a drop down in league, it meant that I would have to do less training, which suited me, and I also felt I would be putting something back into local football.

You often read about ex-pros being targeted for the rough-house treatment when they drop into non-league football during their twilight days, with the local hard man trying to make a name for himself. In the two seasons I played for Haverfordwest and Morriston, I never felt singled out for any particularly bad challenges, and the vast majority of teams tried to play football, although some of the pitches weren't particularly conducive to them being able to do so. I have great memories of playing for both clubs and was treated very well, and I made friends both on and off the park.

At the end of the season, I was quite surprised to receive a call from Neil Halloran at Barry, who asked me to meet and have a chat with him, as he wanted me to rejoin the seaside club. I was a little taken aback, because I was two years older than when I had left them and now nearing forty.

When I'd left Barry, they'd still been in the English pyramid. However, in 1992 they'd been one of the so-called 'Irate Eight', a group of clubs who'd refused to join the newly formed Welsh Premier League. As a result, they'd been forced to play their home games outside Wales at Worcester. After a season of this, the club had realised that it was financially impossible to continue in this manner and had applied to rejoin the Welsh system, where they'd start in the Welsh First Division, one step below the so-called Premier League.

When I met up with the Barry chairman, he explained that the club had pretty much been forced to rejoin the Welsh set-up, and there was a lot of bad feeling amongst the Barry players and the fans at the way they had been treated by the Welsh FA. Neil explained that they were determined to be successful that season and that he hoped I would consider rejoining the club. He said that they hadn't wanted me to leave the club in the first place and that he felt it could be an exciting period in Barry's history.

His words proved to be very prophetic, as during the 1993–94 season we won three trophies, including being promoted to the Welsh Premier League as first-division champions after losing only three games all season. We also won the League Cup and the biggest prize in Welsh Football, the Welsh Cup, which was still a prestigious tournament in those days. The final was a memorable one, as we beat Cardiff City 2–1 at the National Stadium in front of 14,500 fans. Given the fact I was forty and playing for a non-league club, it was probably my favourite of the five Welsh Cups I won as a player.

I then played for the first few months of the following season, including a first-round 7–0 defeat to the Lithuanian cup winners FC Vilnius. This highlighted one of the problems Barry was going to face if they were going to make progress. Even if they were continually dominant in Wales, progress would only be measured by European success, and the gulf in ability was only accentuated by the fact that these European games were usually played in late June or early July before most non-league teams had even started pre-season.

The club then took the very bold step of announcing that they would be the first Welsh non-league team to go full-time. I thought this was a very progressive and brave move, but it also signalled to me that it was time to call my happy period with the club to an end.

Initially, the decision to turn professional helped the club to dominate Welsh football, but European success still proved elusive. And even in their late-1990s heyday, crowds would rarely surpass the 500-mark. With the wage bill of a professional club, it proved almost impossible to maintain a successful squad and remain financially viable. In 2002, John Fashanu took over as manager, and he made headlines with initial promises of African and Chinese TV deals and an influx of Nigerian internationals, but his interest seemed to subside when he had a very successful appearance on ITV's *I'm a Celebrity, Get Me Out of Here*. By the time he left the club, Barry were in a perilous financial state, and in the summer of 2003 they went into administration, with debts approaching £1 million. They were subsequently relegated to the third tier of the Welsh pyramid for the first time. However, in 2008 the club were promoted to the Welsh First Division, and it seems that a quick return to the Welsh Premier Division is on the cards. I hope so, as Barry is a good club with a proud non-league tradition.

By the mid-1990s, I had returned to the Vetch to work as the football in the community officer, and I was getting more involved with the youth-team coaching as well, so it seemed a natural time to concentrate on developing my non-playing career. My appearances on the field over the next few years were confined to representing my local club Mumbles Rangers in the Swansea Senior League. The club is a very friendly one and has a very proud history. It was set up in 1949 by local lad Billy Johns, who despite being confined to a wheelchair as a youngster organised and ran the team until his untimely death at the age of only 33. The club has built on the solid foundations that Billy laid and now has over one hundred and fifty playing members, with three senior teams and a thriving youth section, including teams at Under-10 to Under-16 levels.

I was very pleased to have played for the club at the same time as my two sons, Ian and Gareth, although I knew it was time to finally pack away my boots when at the age of forty-six the rest of the team willingly joined in with their banter that perhaps Gramps needed a chair to sit on during the on-pitch half-time team talks. I have kept a close association with the club since and help out with pre-season training whenever I can. I also usually attend the end-of-season presentation evening.

My rare appearances on the pitch these days are confined to representing the Swansea All Stars in charity matches. I completely refute the rumour spread by Wyndham that I won't play unless I am given the Man of the Match award before each game! We have a great laugh, and although we only play friendlies the old competitive spirit is hard to forget. I think our unbeaten record now stretches back to the mid-1980s. Even though we only play a few times a season, we all look forward to these occasions very much. It's a good way of keeping in touch with all the lads, and I hope I've got a few more games in me yet.

10

RED DRAGON

The summer of 1976, the hottest in recorded history in the UK, might trigger nostalgic recollections of plagues of ladybirds, the hastily drafted drought bill, long queues at standpipes in many places in Wales and, of course, the government's advice that everybody should share a bath in order to save water. But the summer of 1976 is still clearly etched on my memory, not just because the temperature in early May nearly touched 30 degrees Celsius. Between 24 April and 22 May, I played in five full internationals for Wales, having only just gained my first cap against England that March. If some of today's internationals complain of burn-out, can you imagine what they would have made of launching straight into such a programme of competitive football at the end of the domestic season without any rest period?

However, I was in my element. Not only had I just fulfilled my ambition of breaking into the national team, but it was a perfect time to do so, as Wales had just qualified for the quarter-finals of the European Championships, although I can't personally claim any credit for the fact that the Red Dragons had emerged top of a difficult qualifying group that had included Austria and Hungary, who were at that time much stronger powers in the European game than they are today.

The 1976 European Championships was the last time that the tournament was played under the old format, which meant that only four teams qualified for the finals. By 1980 (four years too late for us), the eight group winners obtained a place in the finals, and this was increased to sixteen teams by Euro 96 in England. Commentators often repeat the old chestnut that Wales have failed to qualify for a major tournament since 1958. In his autobiography, Terry Yorath argued that the 1976 team had qualified for the finals by winning their group and that it was only the format of the competition at that time that prevented them from taking their place in a major tournament.

I also think people often forget that the famous 1958 team didn't actually qualify for the World Cup finals initially, but won a play-off against Israel after coming second in their group. In the Asia-Africa qualifying group, none of the Arab teams would play against Israel, so FIFA decided that they should face a play-off against one of the runners-up from the European groups to see who qualified. When the draw was made, Wales came out of the hat and subsequently beat the Israelis 4–0 on aggregate to qualify for Sweden. I don't think that this fact actually detracts from the performance of the team at the finals, and if John Charles had played against Brazil, Wales might even have gone all the way to the final and won it. At the end of the day, whether you think it was important how we qualified is up to each individual's own interpretation. What is certain is that I had become a member of a team that contained many great players, one that I feel can be classified as amongst Wales's greatest ever.

We had been given one of the toughest draws in the quarter-finals, being paired with a very strong Yugoslavia. They were technically a very good side but also had a reputation for rugged and sometimes overly rigorous play. Mike Smith, the Wales manager, said, 'To say that the Yugoslavians were a hard side is putting it mildly.' But we weren't intimidated, and it was also drummed into us not to retaliate at any cost, although keeping to that instruction would be fully put to the test over the two legs.

The first game was to be played at the Maksimir Stadium, Zagreb, on 24 April 1976, with a crowd of well over 50,000 expected. We flew out to Yugoslavia on the Friday, mainly because some of the squad had been forced to play for their clubs on the Wednesday night. Despite the fact that we were the only British team to qualify, there was no attempt by the league clubs to allow our players to have a clear week off before such an important game.

On the morning of the match, I was told by manager Mike Smith that I would be one of the four substitutes, and Brian Flynn was selected to take up a place in a strong midfield alongside Terry Yorath and John Mahoney. Our success as a team was based on excellent team spirit and our great national fervour to represent our country. Also, unlike many Wales teams both past and present, our squad contained a majority of players who were playing on a regular basis for their First Division clubs. As well as the three midfielders mentioned, our squad had players of the calibre of John Toshack and Joey Jones of Liverpool, Leighton James and Rod Thomas of Derby, Leighton Phillips of Aston Villa and Dai Davies of Everton.

The game started in the worst possible fashion, as we conceded a sloppy goal after only 40 seconds. The Yugoslavs kicked off, and Terry Yorath slipped as he went to challenge their striker, whose shot was saved by Dai Davies only to rebound straight to Momčilo Vukotić, who put us one behind. For the remainder of the game, we matched them across the centre two-thirds of the pitch but didn't really create many clear-cut chances and failed to break down the tough Eastern European defence. We went two down on the hour, again after another defensive error. We failed to clear our lines, and Branko Oblak's cross was turned in by Danilo Popivoda.

I was pleased to come on as a substitute for Leighton James but a little disappointed to only get six minutes at the end of the game.

Despite only being on the pitch for a short time, their left-back gave me a hell of a whack the first time I touched the ball. Four years later, I looked up at training one day to see our new signing was the very same player, staring at me with a knowing smile on his face. It was, of course, Jimmy Hadžiabdić. Unfortunately, in the early 1990s Jimmy had to flee with his family from his home in Mostar, Bosnia, due to the conflict, and they had to leave all their possessions behind. When we met up after he moved back to Swansea, I remembered that I had swapped a jersey with another one of his teammates after the Yugoslavia match in Cardiff, and I know Jimmy really appreciated it when I gave it to him.

Before the return leg, we had to negotiate the annual Home International Championship, which had been played over eight days every May since 1969. This gave Welsh and Northern Irish players a chance to pit themselves against the Scots and, of course, the English. The championships kicked off for us on a Thursday night at the famous Hampden Park in Glasgow. Despite the reputation that the venue had for the famous 'Hampden Roar', the game was played in a fairly subdued atmosphere in front of a crowd of barely 10,000. Perhaps the home fans had been deterred by the line-ups, as both Scotland and Wales fielded what could be perceived as reserve teams. Mike Smith had 'rested' eight of the side that had started in Zagreb, and it was no surprise that we went down 3–1.

Although we lost, I felt that I had done OK, and somebody later showed me the *Western Mail* match report, which reported, 'Curtis displayed both courage and skill battling up front on his own against a tough defence for much of the game.' Although the praise was naturally very nice, I certainly didn't let it inflate my ego, because even at the age of only 21 I knew not to believe my own press too much, as the next headline could often be much less complimentary.

Two days later, we were back in Wales to face England at Ninian Park, and I was again picked in the starting XI in a more familiar-looking line-up, similar to the one that had faced Yugoslavia. In a very even game, we matched a strong England team, and I felt we were unlucky to go down to a solitary goal from Peter Taylor on the hour. After being substituted in the 78th minute, I have to admit I was shattered, as I had played virtually two full internationals within forty-eight hours, which was certainly a step up from the pace of Fourth Division football with the Swans.

After the game, Mike Smith pulled me aside and told me I had done really well and that I would be keeping my starting place for the following Friday's game against Northern Ireland. I was obviously pleased to keep my place but more so because the game was due to be played at my home ground. Although the match itself was pretty nondescript, we did at least get back to winning ways, edging past the Irish with a Leighton James goal. My favourite memory of the game was the massive roar that emanated from the North Bank every time I touched the ball, filling me with a huge sense of pride and rounding off what had been a great week in my career.

The return leg against the Yugoslavs was to be played a few weeks later on 22 May in Cardiff. On the Friday night, Mike Smith talked to all the players individually. When he came to me, he said that although he had been very impressed with my performances so far, he was opting for Brian Flynn and Tosh up front. Although I tried very hard to mask my feelings, I think Smith could tell I was quite upset. Perhaps he thought that playing Brian alongside John would replicate the great success that Liverpool had in the mid-1970s when Kevin Keegan so successfully partnered the big man, winning trophies both domestically and in Europe.

Funnily enough, although Brian and I later played a lot of internationals together, we never really talk about the old games when we meet up now to work with the Wales squads at Under-21 or Under-19 levels. Instead, in training or during a match one of us will say doesn't so-and-so remind you a lot of the way one of our international colleagues played when we were with Wales. For example, both of us think that Andrew Crofts of Gillingham plays very much like ex-Stoke and Wales star John Mahoney.

If Smith's selection of the five-foot-three-inch Flynn as a striker had been somewhat of a talking point, this paled into insignificance compared with the controversy that surrounded the game itself. After the rough-house tactics in Zagreb, the game was obviously not going to be played in a Corinthian spirit, and the atmosphere was made more intense by the passionate home crowd. In those days, the pitch at Ninian Park was surrounded by huge fencing on three sides, making the fans feel penned in. This and the alcohol that was freely allowed into the ground was often a recipe for trouble. Immediately after the game kicked off, the two teams went at each other, and the tackles flew as the pitch resembled more of a battlefield than a football match. The referee Rudi Glöckner was supposed to be highly experienced, having taken charge of the 1970 World Cup final, but he also had a reputation for arrogance and was sometimes criticised for his overtly flamboyant style. As if playing up to this reputation, Glöckner awarded the Yugoslavs a very dubious penalty against Malcolm Page in the 19th minute, despite the fact that Popivoda stumbled and clearly caused Page to fall over in the box before theatrically throwing himself over the prostrate defender. The home crowd's mood was not improved a moment later when Josip Katalinski buried the spot-kick to put them three up on aggregate. In fact, the litany of on-field fouls was now being matched by the array of coins and bottles being thrown from the terraces, especially at the Grange End of the ground. However, the tension in the crowd abated for a while when our defender Ian Evans got an equaliser close to half-time.

Early in the second half, things again turned nasty after what seemed a perfectly good goal from Tosh was disallowed by the referee for what he claimed was a high foot from John Mahoney earlier in the move. Glöckner's decision caused a near riot, with some fans climbing over the fences, and there seemed to be a genuine threat of a pitch invasion. I was warming up on the touchline at the time, ready to come on, and I heard the referee tell both managers that he was very close to abandoning the match. Play eventually restarted after a break of six minutes, and I came on in place of Wrexham's Arfon Griffiths.

On the pitch, the controversy continued as we pressurised the away team and came very close to getting the two goals we needed to force a replay. Not only was another Toshack effort ruled out for an offside decision that was debatable to say the least, but with ten minutes to go we were awarded a penalty that Terry Yorath unfortunately missed. Who knows what would have happened if we had gone 2–1 up. I thought that the Yugoslavs were beginning to buckle, and I'm sure we could have got another. However, there's no way that Terry should be blamed for the miss, as Arfon, our regular penalty taker, was off the pitch, and two senior players who were regular penalty takers for their clubs refused to take it. In the end, the result was frustrating and left a feeling of if only. I didn't know it at the time, but this was not the last time that I was going to be left with such feelings after an international match for Wales.

The disappointments against Yugoslavia were yet to come when I'd made my debut against England only two months previously. The game was played to celebrate the Welsh FA's centenary, and although officially a friendly, a game against England is no such thing, as any Welshman would tell you. Two days before the match, there was the usual withdrawal of players from both squads, and when both John Toshack and Leighton James pulled out I thought I had a good chance of making my debut. In fact, both Carl Harris, the teenager from Neath who had just broken into the Leeds first team, and I were selected to win our first caps in front of a crowd of nearly 21,000 at the Racecourse, Wrexham. The Racecourse was a ground where Wales had a very good record, perhaps because the fans were so close to the pitch. With 20,000-plus crowded onto the terraces, it was an intimidating place for opponents to come. I was, of course, very proud to run out to win my first cap, but I was more pleased for my family, as I knew it meant a lot to them that I had followed in Uncle Roy's footsteps.

The game itself was typical of any between the old rivals: competitive and tough. Although Don Revie's team had suffered from several withdrawals, it still included household names such as Kevin Keegan, Mick Channon, Trevor Brooking and both Liverpool Rays, Kennedy and Clemence. We matched England until the final quarter when they went ahead with goals by Kennedy and Peter Taylor. My own magic moment came in the final minute when I was in the right place to tap in after a goalmouth scramble. In fact, I could have scored two, as in the 57th minute John Roberts headed a Terry Yorath free-kick into my path. The ball sat up perfectly for me to hit on the half-volley, and I was sure it was heading for the top corner until their defender Mike Doyle got in the way and it hit him square in the face. I must have struck it quite well, as it took him a few minutes to come round. As well as being delighted with my goal, I had a few good runs. Overall, I was quite pleased with my debut and didn't feel out of place against opposition players who all played in a division three above that of my own club.

During the post-match meal, it was announced that the Wales players were to be presented with a special memento of the occasion. As I queued, I was getting quite excited thinking about what we were going to get: perhaps a decanter or maybe an engraved pewter jug? When I was about halfway down the line, I could see that a few of my teammates had opened their packages. Some were shaking their heads and a couple had wry smiles on their faces. When I received my memento and opened it, the reason for the lads' reactions became very apparent. We had each been given a set of four plastic-coated tea coasters emblazoned with the Welsh FA logo. As I was to find out over the next ten years, the Wales players were not always the first priority of the Welsh FA.

I was much happier when I arrived back in Pentre at about 3 a.m.

after a long, exhausting and emotional day to be greeted by the sight of the village decorated with flags, bunting and a big sign that read 'Congratulations Alan on winning your first cap'. I was lucky, though, because the following year during the Queen's Silver Jubilee, when every Valley town had a street party, the village ran out of bunting and had to improvise by using women's underwear instead. I'm not sure what message I would have got if they had done that for me after the England game!

If the 1976 European Championship play-offs had given me a tantalising glimpse of international football at its highest level, it had also exposed me to the first of many set-backs that the team would suffer in qualifying tournaments over the following decade. The qualifying rounds for the 1978 World Cup finals proved to be the start of an unparalleled period of both success and frustration for Welsh football. Between 1978 and 1986, we came agonisingly close to qualifying for four of the five tournaments we entered, only to fall at the final hurdle on every occasion.

Many of these campaigns are best remembered for their moments of controversy, none more so than the campaign to qualify for the World Cup in Argentina in 1978. We were drawn in a three-team pool with Czechoslovakia and familiar foes Scotland, with only the top team going to South America. The fact that there were only three countries in the group actually served to increase the pressure, as each fixture was like a cup final. Compare this with today when some qualifying groups have seven or eight teams and a nation can lose its first three or four games but still qualify.

I think the overall standard of international football has improved over the years, as teams such as Cyprus, Malta and Luxembourg are now much more organised and harder to beat. What is perhaps most significant is that the number of international teams has increased dramatically, and there are therefore more countries with similar-sized populations and playing standards as Wales. Although Italy, Spain, Germany and Holland are still the dominant nations, the USSR and Yugoslavia, who were themselves powers in the European game, have been replaced by over 20 new countries. Inevitably, Wales play more games against teams who are on a par with us, and the results of many internationals today are much harder to predict.

The first qualifying fixture of the campaign saw us face Scotland at Hampden Park in November 1976 in front of 63,000 at the famous old stadium, over 50,000 more fans than had turned up for the Home International Championship fixture the previous May. We lost 1–0 to an Ian Evans own goal after only 15 minutes, and despite going close a few times we couldn't get the crucial equaliser. I came off the bench for Leighton James with 20 minutes to go. There was really nothing between the teams, and a draw would probably have been a fair result.

Although I was disappointed with the result, I felt I had come a long way in my international career in a short time, having played in eight consecutive internationals. So it came as quite a bombshell to be dropped for the first time in my international career when the squad was announced for the first home game of the group against Czechoslovakia in March 1977. I was upset to be left out, as I was scoring regularly for the Swans in a team pushing for promotion and felt that I had made a valid contribution to the Wales team in all my appearances the previous year.

I was obviously very disappointed, but I did suspect that it might happen at some time, as I figured it would be easier for Mike to leave out somebody who played in the Fourth Division as opposed to a more seasoned pro with a First Division team. I have to say that Mike never actually made me feel that this was the case and that the other players in the squad were always great with me. I enjoyed playing under Mike Smith, and I found him to be a very genuine guy whom I believe did a lot for Welsh football.

The fact that we beat the Czechs 3–0 was a double-edged sword: of course I wanted my team to win, but I knew that a good victory would only make my chances of being selected for the next game even tougher.

Being recalled to the squad for the Home International Championship of 1977 and featuring as a substitute in draws against Northern Ireland and Scotland gave me some encouragement that I could win back my place. That tournament also gave rise to one of the few real regrets of my Wales career: that I didn't play in the game against England. I sat on the bench and watched as a Leighton James penalty gave us our first-ever victory at Wembley. From a personal viewpoint, I was as delighted as anybody with our victory, but my happiness was also tinged with a little sadness. Wales hadn't beaten England since 1955, and a key member of the Wales team that day had been my uncle Roy. As I celebrated with the lads at the final whistle, I thought that it would have been nice to have shared some of that history with him.

Although we didn't lose a game, we were pipped to the championship by Scotland, who also came away from Wembley with a famous victory. However, unlike the celebrations of the Wales players at the end of the game, the Scotland players were infamously joined on the pitch by thousands of their fans, many of whom decided to make souvenirs of the Wembley turf and goalposts. Some observers have suggested that this game and the Scotland fans' behaviour marked the beginning of the end of the Home International Championship.

There has been some talk in the press of the competition being brought back, especially after none of the home nations qualified for Euro 2008. I don't feel this would serve any great benefit, as I don't think players would really learn anything from the experience. If British teams insist on playing international friendlies, they should at least take on Continental teams and learn to adapt to different styles of play. I'm not sure many players or their managers would see the benefit of three or four physical local derbies at the end of an already long season. It will be interesting to see how many of the league clubs will make their star players available if the provisionally approved

Celtic League between Wales, Northern Ireland, the Republic of Ireland and Scotland actually starts in 2011.

If the Scottish fans had created a hostile atmosphere at Wembley, it was nothing compared to the intimidating atmosphere that faced the Wales players in the return World Cup qualifier. The Welsh FA in their infinite wisdom had decided to play the game not at the Racecourse, where we had a very good record, but 30 miles down the road at Anfield. I think they thought this would be a far greater money-spinner, as they could get three times the crowd at Liverpool's ground. It turned out to be a disastrous decision that really backfired on the team. After the close game at Hampden, we felt we could turn over the Scots at home, but the Welsh FA's decision to change the venue completely scuppered any psychological edge that a home fixture normally provides.

As we looked around the ground during the pre-match kickabout, all we could see was a sea of blue shirts and tartan. Tosh turned to me and said, 'Aren't we supposed to be the home team?' In fact, we had some indication of the atmosphere to expect when the coach pulled up outside the ground and all we could see were Scotland fans. Actually, we could hear them shouting abuse, but we couldn't really see them, as the coach quickly became drowned in spittle. Anfield, therefore, was packed to the rafters with Scotland fans, who had managed to get their hands on the vast majority of tickets and must have outnumbered the Wales supporters by more than eight to one.

With ten minutes to go, the game was evenly poised, with both sides having come close to taking the lead, when Willie Johnston launched a hopeful cross into our box. Our defender David Jones and Scotland centre-forward Joe Jordan jumped for the ball with their hands above their heads. Referee Robert Wirtz adjudged that it was definitely a red-shirted sleeve that had hit it and gave a penalty. Was he influenced by the shouts from the crowd? I'm not sure.

Although Jordan still categorically denies it was his arm that struck the ball, the more times I see the incident on TV the more convinced

I am that it was a blue arm that made contact with it. I shared a room with Joe for a year at Southampton, but I never actually tackled him about the incident, although I was present on several occasions when others did ask him about it, and he denied it more vigorously every time the subject was raised. He took the same line in his recent autobiography.

After Don Masson had struck home the penalty, our heads dropped, and a Kenny Dalglish header made the result safe for the Scots, who were then favourites to reach Argentina. Scotland subsequently beat the Czechs at home to qualify as group winners, whilst we lost to them 1–0 away, a game I missed due to an illness in the family.

The fact that both the Yugoslavia result of 1976 and the Scottish game at Anfield produced such controversy seems to have cast a shadow over Welsh football. The Wales international team developed a reputation for somehow contriving to blow our chances at the last moment when qualification for a major tournament seemed well within our grasp. This notion of a team destined to fail at the last hurdle in qualification due to a bad refereeing decision, a controversial moment or simply bad luck was one that seemed only to be fuelled by the events of subsequent qualifying tournaments. What I would certainly refute is the allegation in some quarters that we somehow bottled it on the big occasions. I believe we had a good enough team to qualify, but we never had the strength in depth to absorb injuries to key players. Also, I can't imagine there were many other teams who suffered from as many controversial refereeing decisions or failed to get the rub of the green as many times as we did. There are some conspiracy theorists who might argue that the luck and refereeing decisions always went against us because we are a small and unfashionable nation, but I think that would be virtually impossible to prove either way.

Having said that, the campaign for qualification for the European Championship in Belgium in 1980 was probably the only time that we didn't live up to this 'nearly man' tag during my time with the national team. I missed the first two home qualifying games at Wrexham against Malta and Turkey before Christmas due to a stomach-muscle tear. The Malta game was a particularly bad one to miss for a striker, as we won 7–0 at a time when Wales rarely won by such scores at international level.

The qualification place was really going to be decided by our head-to-head with the all-powerful West Germany team. I was fit again and selected in the starting line-up for the home game against the Germans the following May. In their qualifying games, the previously consistent German team had been anything but, only just scraping a goalless draw away against the Turks and, more surprisingly, the same result in Valetta against lowly ranked Malta. However, on the night we seemed to freeze as if too impressed by their reputation rather than their current form, and we allowed their midfielder Uli Stielike of Real Madrid to dominate the game. During the second half, the Wales team included a record four players from the Swans, which highlighted the growing reputation that the West Wales club was gaining at that time under the stewardship of John Toshack.

When I next played for Wales, a week later in a 3–0 victory over Scotland in the Home International Championship, I completed another record, being one of four Leeds United players in the team, along with the late Byron Stevenson, Carl Harris and Brian Flynn. I don't know whether it was the adrenalin caused by the transfer activity during that week or the exciting prospect of playing in the First Division, but this was by far the best game I had played for my country up to that point. The following Monday, Karl Woodward wrote, 'The brilliantly inventive Curtis was involved in all three of Wales's goals and is worth every penny of the huge fee Leeds paid for him.' I think that this report cost me a small fortune, as I ended up buying Karl a few pints every time our paths crossed after that match!

We drew the next two games, with an excellent goalless draw at Wembley against England and a 1–1 draw against Northern Ireland at Windsor Park, which was always a tough away fixture. Despite being pipped again for the Home International Championship, this time by England, we travelled to Malta at the end of the week in good heart for the next European Championship qualifier. We secured a comfortable 2–0 victory despite playing in furnace-like conditions on a horrendously rutted and rock-solid pitch – probably the worst I had ever played on in senior football. Having experienced the conditions in Valetta for ourselves, it became apparent why the Germans had only scraped a draw there.

Both the team and I approached the away fixture in Germany with some confidence. We were unbeaten in five games, and I had played in six consecutive matches, having scored in my last appearance in a 2–1 win over the Republic of Ireland in a friendly at the Vetch in September. We went into the game at the Müngersdorfer Stadion in Cologne two points ahead of our opponents, with a far superior goal difference, so a draw would have been a good result. But the match turned out to be a disaster, as we were hammered 5–1 on a miserable night. It was the worst result for Wales for 26 years. Even my second goal in two international matches, when I intercepted a poor backpass by Herbert Zimmerman with four minutes to go, didn't help lift the feeling of embarrassment at our performance.

Our mood wasn't improved in the final qualifier when we went down by a solitary goal to Turkey in Izmir. The game was played in a smouldering atmosphere, filled with menace. As we came out of the dressing-rooms, we had an inclination of what to expect when we had to pass through a tunnel of hundreds of army conscripts to enter the playing arena, apparently for our own safety. Despite the presence of so many policemen and soldiers, it didn't stop the Turkish fans from pelting us throughout the game with coins and other missiles. The referee was completely intimidated and allowed the Turks to get away with a series of over-the-top fouls, late tackles, body checks and shirt pulling. In the 68th minute, Byron Stevenson retaliated to yet another foul and was sent off for punching, which was completely out of character for him. After that, the referee gave every decision to our opponents, and it was no surprise when they scored with ten minutes to go. To be honest, by the time the final whistle went we were just glad to get off the pitch in one piece. In what was to become a familiar picture in Turkey, we were escorted off under the shields of the military police and army. Both UEFA and FIFA did nothing against the home side, although Byron got a four-year ban from all UEFA-run competitions.

In the past 25 years, the experiences of away teams and fans in Turkey have only worsened, culminating in the sad deaths of two Leeds fans in Istanbul in 2000. In fact, it wasn't until 2005, when there were pitched battles between Swiss and Turkish players in the World Cup play-offs, that FIFA actually did anything to punish Turkey and their fans.

Despite the defeats to West Germany and Turkey, we felt we were rebuilding as a team and could make the final push to qualification for the next World Cup in Spain. I finally felt confident that I had established myself as an international footballer, having played in the last eight matches, and that at the age of twenty-five the move to play First Division football at Leeds would only enhance my prospects at that level.

When the qualifying draw was made for the 1982 World Cup, we were grouped with Iceland, USSR, Czechoslovakia and Turkey again. Although by no means an easy group, we felt we had a genuine chance of qualification, and I was looking forward to the challenge. As 1979 turned into 1980, I could look back on the best year of my career and felt that things could only get better at club and international level. However, on 5 January 1980 everything changed when I suffered my career-threatening injury in the clash with Peter Shilton. The injury had a dramatic impact upon my international career. It was exactly 21 months later that I was to next pull on the red shirt of my country. Serious injuries never happen at a good time, but the timing of mine seemed particularly disastrous.

By then, Mike England had replaced Mike Smith as manager of the national team, and there was the danger that being out of sight could be tantamount to being out of mind with the new manager. At least Smith had picked me 20 times for Wales already and knew what I was capable of, especially as he had also been my manager in the Welsh youth set-up, but England would perhaps have his own ideas and want to select different players.

During my time out of the game injured, I missed the 1980 Home International Championship, including the famous 4–1 demolition of England at Wrexham, but more importantly I missed the 4–0 win in the qualifying tie against Iceland in Reykjavik as England began to assemble a squad to challenge for qualification for Spain. Not only was the team taking shape, but new players were challenging for the forward positions, including a young Liverpool striker called Ian Rush and Ian Walsh, then playing with Palace in the top division.

By the time I returned to fitness at Leeds, the manager at Elland Road had also changed, and I was in and out of the team, a fact that I'm sure didn't help my chances of being picked for Wales. In the autumn of 1980, I missed out on selection for the home qualifying wins against Turkey and Czechoslovakia, and again missed out the following spring as the team beat Turkey in the away fixture. This was probably the most frustrating time of my career. I was struggling at club and international level, but the team were flying. Being a proud Welshman, I wanted to be part of it. There is no doubt that the move back to the Vetch helped rebuild my international career, even though the main reason for the transfer was for me to get regular first-team football.

In fact, by the time I was recalled to the Wales squad for the Home International Championship of 1981, I had been out of the national team for seventeen months and had missed eight games, including four consecutive World Cup qualifying wins. Mike England hadn't picked me once, and when questioned by the press about this he told them that he felt my spell at Leeds had significantly impacted on my performances but added that my recent form with the Swans had warranted my return to the squad. 'Alan has been playing like his old self in the past couple of months and is one of the main reasons why the Swans were able to clinch promotion to the First Division,' he said.

I was raring to prove to England what I could do, so was a little frustrated not to get a run-out in the home victory over Scotland or the goalless draw against England at Wembley. However, it looked as if I would be selected for the game against Northern Ireland in Belfast and finally get the chance to restart my international career. At that time, the Troubles were at their height, and the death of IRA hunger striker Bobby Sands had only served to exacerbate the tension and threat of violence. A few days before the match, the Welsh FA announced that they would be following the English FA in withdrawing from the fixture for safety reasons, and my comeback was delayed.

After not featuring in any of Mike England's teams thus far, I wasn't surprised to be left out for the next qualifier against the Soviets, which we drew 0–0. I have to admit that during this period I did wonder whether I would break back into the team at all. The manager could argue that he had only lost twice in eleven games, and without me the team had scored nine goals in five qualifiers, remaining unbeaten in the group.

Even though Mike England didn't pick me when he initially became Welsh manager, I think this was more to do with the fact that I had been out of the game for so long rather than any opinion he had of me as a player. Mike was a really genuine guy and had been an outstanding centre-back with both Blackburn and Spurs in his day. He could also be quite eccentric, and he would often forget players' names, especially those of our opponents. In a friendly against France in the early 1980s, he told Mickey Thomas that he should keep a close eye on their midfielder with the curly hair. When Mickey, with tongue firmly in cheek, asked him which one, Mike replied, 'You know. The guy who's always on the telly.'

After a few minutes of this, Mickey turned to Mike and said, 'Do you mean Michel Platini?'

Stony-faced, Mike replied, 'Yes, that's the fella.'

One of my favourite memories of Mike is from when I first returned to the squad. He was very complimentary about me during my first training session and kept shouting 'DK, Curt' or 'DK, son' every time I touched the ball. At the end of the session, I had to ask, 'What does "DK" mean, boss?'

Without batting an eyelid, Mike replied, 'Different class, son! Different class.' Every time I think of this story, it makes me smile, even today.

It was going to be vital that I hit the ground running at the start of the 1981–82 campaign with the Swans and prove second time around that I could perform in the top division of English football. The fact that we had a flying start to our first-ever campaign at that level and topped the table in the first weeks of the season couldn't have come at a better time for my international prospects. Mike England was at the famous 5–1 win over Leeds, and he must have been impressed, as he picked me to face the Czechs in the early September qualifier in Prague.

When I ran out at the Rošický Stadium to win my twenty-first cap, it had been almost two years since my last appearance for my country. I couldn't have picked a much tougher game to have made my comeback in, as the Czechs were a very strong side and had a good manager in Dr Josef Vengloš, later to go on to manage Aston Villa and Celtic. It was important that we keep it tight at the back, and we initially did so, absorbing a lot of pressure until conceding a freak own goal in the 25th minute. The Czech midfielder Antonín Panenka whipped a free-kick into the box, which Byron Stevenson tried to clear only to direct the ball towards his own goal, where it hit the post. Dai Davies tried to gather the rebound but only succeeded in deflecting the ball back into the net.

I had to feel sorry for Dai. He got a lot of flak for it in the press, who quickly forgot that up to that point he had gone five qualifying games without conceding a goal. Like his predecessor in the Wales goal, Gary Sprake, Dai had gained an unfair reputation for making errors in crucial games. I think that both keepers proved themselves week in week out to be outstanding and that goalkeepers by nature of their position make errors that usually result in goals, whilst those of outfield players are easily overlooked. As a striker, if I missed three easy chances but scored the winning goal in the last minute, I would be a hero. I definitely wouldn't have wanted to be a goalkeeper.

By the time the Czechs had scored their second in the 67th minute, it would be fair to say that we were well beaten and were somewhat relieved not to concede another. Although I was delighted to be back playing at international level, it hadn't been the comeback that I had really envisaged after two years out of the team. Despite the defeat by the Czechs, we still headed the group by one point, with what seemed a relatively easy home game against Iceland to follow. The Icelanders were not the strongest of teams, especially away from home, and had conceded eighteen goals in six qualifying games, including the four unanswered ones we had scored against them in Reykjavik. With two further points in the bag, we hoped to travel to the Soviet Union only needing a draw or, if other results went in our favour, even a narrow defeat to qualify for Spain.

It was on 14 October 1981 at the Vetch Field that another chapter was written in the saga of Wales's attempts to qualify for a major tournament. This was the night that the lights literally went out on our chances of qualifying for the following year's World Cup finals. Mike England had picked an attacking formation that included six Swansea players on our home ground. From the kick-off, we got at the Icelanders and squandered a series of good chances, only converting one by Robbie James in the twenty-fifth minute. As the interval approached, our thoughts turned to the likely bollocking we were going to get from the manager for having failed to extend our solitary-goal lead. With less than a minute to go before the referee blew his whistle, the ground was plunged into almost complete darkness when all four floodlights failed. When enough power was eventually restored to continue play, we had been off the field for 42 minutes. It was slightly surreal to watch the Finnish referee Arto Ravander play the last few seconds of the first half before blowing up and making us immediately switch ends to kick off the second period.

The disruption had clearly affected us, as the Icelanders went straight up the field and equalised in what was probably their first serious attack. Even though I scored to put us 2–1 up after fifty-four minutes, our second-half performance was disjointed, and they drew level again five minutes later when Ásgeir Sigurvinsson of Bayern Munich got his second. Despite bringing on Ian Rush as an extra attacker, we just couldn't seem to recapture our rhythm of the first half, and in fairness to them they defended really well in the last half hour. As far as I was concerned, the bizarre incident of the floodlights failing had certainly dimmed our World Cup hopes, if not completely pulled the plug on them. In hindsight, rather than playing so many attacking players, we would have been better off settling for a 1–0 or 2–1 win, which would have probably given us enough points to qualify. Now we had to travel over 2,500 miles to play the USSR in harsh winter conditions in Tbilisi, needing a win to definitely guarantee qualification.

By late November in Georgia, the conditions were well below freezing, and with 80,000 fanatical fans behind them the game was over by the 20th minute when their star player Oleg Blokhin put them 2–0 up. We were eventually well beaten 3–0. The Soviets had won the group, but we still had a chance of qualifying as runners-up if they could beat the Czechs in the final game. Even though the Soviets were more than capable of winning the match, we weren't holding our breath that they would do us a favour and put out a fellow Eastern bloc nation. It was all but predictable ten days later when the USSR and Czechoslovakia drew 1–1 in an atmosphere described by some commentators as being more akin to an exhibition match. We had failed to qualify at the last hurdle again, and it especially hurt, as England, Scotland and Northern Ireland all made it to the finals. It might be all ifs and buts now, but I'm sure that if we had beaten the Icelanders by a couple of goals at the Vetch, we would have qualified for Spain.

After the disappointment of failing to qualify for the 1982 World Cup, we were given another tough task for the 1984 European Championships, being grouped with two more Eastern European teams, Yugoslavia and Bulgaria, plus the ever-improving Norway. We started the group well, with a narrow win over the Norwegians at the Vetch in September 1982. By Christmas of that year, as the next qualifier was approaching, I was increasingly suffering from constant pain in the knee I had injured at Leeds and had to withdraw from the match against Yugoslavia in Titograd (a game which resulted in an amazing 4–4 draw). I was frustrated to have to withdraw from the squad but was even more flabbergasted when I became involved in a club-versus-country row. I had always been proud of representing my country and, unlike some other players, always travelled to internationals, even if I knew I probably wouldn't be selected, so I was really annoyed when the Welsh FA wrote to the Swans asking them for confirmation regarding my withdrawal. The Swansea management wrote back to inform the FA that I was struggling so much that they were only picking me for weekend games and hadn't themselves selected me for two games in a week.

During that period, I was really suffering and was playing with heavy strapping on my knee, which was so painful that I was barely training in the week, if at all. When I was forced to withdraw from the February 1983 game against England and the 1–0 qualifying win over Bulgaria in March, I knew I would have a huge struggle on my hands to get back into the international squad. In fact, I only played once in 1983, in a friendly against Romania, when I scored after coming off the bench. I wasn't selected to play in any further

European qualifiers, and once again Wales failed to qualify, coming runners-up to Yugoslavia by a single point.

By the time the draw was made for the qualifiers for the 1986 World Cup in Mexico, I was nearly 31 and thought that it was probably going to be my last shot at appearing in a major tournament with Wales. I had been on the fringes of the squad for the previous two years and realised that I had to perform to a consistently high standard at club level to win back my place in Mike England's team. At that time, I had just made the move to Southampton, and I think the higher profile coverage of the First Division certainly helped bring me back to the attention of the Wales manager.

Our start to the campaign was dreadful, losing away to Iceland, and we were well beaten by Spain in my comeback game in Seville. Having played two games and lost them both, our chances of qualification seemed slim to say the least. I didn't make the starting line-up for the next two qualifiers, but we increased our chances of making it to Mexico with a great 1–0 victory over the Scots at Hampden and a famous 3–0 home defeat of Spain. I knew that with Mark Hughes and Ian Rush in great form up front, it was going to be difficult to dislodge either of them from the team, especially as Ian had scored the winner in Glasgow and Sparky had scored a wonder goal with an overhead scissor-kick from outside the box against Spain. However, I was playing well for the Saints, and when I was selected to start in both friendly matches against Norway either side of the Spain game, I knew I was still clearly in the manager's thoughts. If we qualified for the finals, I thought I would have an excellent chance of being on the plane to Mexico.

Not for the first time, our qualification rested on the last game of the group when we faced Scotland at home on 10 September 1985, but unlike in 1977 the crowd would be mostly Wales fans at Ninian Park. If we won the match, we would qualify, banishing the memories of the handball incident at Anfield and nearly a decade of close calls and controversial heartache. Surely there couldn't be any more twists to the story of Wales's attempts to qualify for a major tournament.

On the evening of 10 September 1985, in front of a packed crowd of 40,000 at Ninian Park, we firmly believed that it was going to be our time. The game started at a high tempo, and Mark Hughes and Ian Rush gave the Scotland defence a torrid time, especially Sparky with his physicality. The home crowd exploded after only 14 minutes when Hughes gave us the lead with a typically brilliant strike. After the Scots had failed to clear a throw-in from the left by Dave Phillips, Peter Nicholas won the ball, and his low cross was met on the volley by the Manchester United striker, who buried the ball in the left-hand corner of Jim Leighton's goal. We dominated the Scots up to half-time but couldn't quite fashion the killer second goal.

The second half started in a similar manner to the first, and in the 55th minute Ian Rush missed a chance that he would normally have buried. Although the tension was obviously rising, we thought we had one foot in Mexico, but fate intervened again, this time in the form of Dutch referee Jan Keizer, who made another terrible refereeing decision, unfortunately not the first in the history of Welsh international football. In the 81st minute, a Steve Nicol cross was flicked on by Graeme Sharp, and David Speedie attempted an overambitious scissor-kick, which rebounded off Dave Phillips, who was standing a yard behind the Scotland striker. Unbelievably, the referee pointed to the spot, and after much protest Davie Cooper converted the penalty. By the time we had recovered from the shock, the referee had blown for full-time.

Mike England summed up what we all felt when he said, 'All the players feel absolutely cheated. The ball was a yard away from David and was blasted at him. How could it possibly have been deliberate hand ball? Once again, a contentious refereeing decision has done so much damage to the cause of Welsh football.'

As we sat in the dressing-room totally gutted, our mood became even more sombre when we were told that the Scotland manager

Jock Stein had died of a heart attack after being carried away from the dug-out with only two minutes of the game left. Jock had been a legendary manager with Celtic and famously brought the European Cup to Glasgow in 1967, making them the first British team to win the trophy. It was a real tragedy. The majority of the Scotland players were in tears after the game, and I think it put our own disappointment into context for us.

After the game against the Scots, I only played twice more for Wales, both in friendlies, one against Hungary in the match immediately after the disappointment of Ninian Park and once two years later at the Vetch, ironically enough whilst I was then a Cardiff City player. In 1987, at the age of thirty-three and carrying a nagging knee injury, I knew that I couldn't go through another two-year qualifying tournament. I did get called up to a few squads after that but never actually played again, although in those days you didn't formally announce your international retirement, you just tended to fade out of the scene. Therefore, I never actually hung up my boots, and as I've told Tosh several times when he's suffered squad withdrawals in recent years, I'm still available if he needs me.

If you had told me when I was a football-mad youngster kicking the ball around the rec in Pentre that I would have won just one cap for Wales, I would have taken that there and then. Anything else was always a bonus. In the final reckoning, I played thirty-five times for Wales and scored six international goals. If I'm critical of myself, I think that I perhaps should have scored a few more goals, but in quite a few games, especially away from home, I was played out wide as part of a five-man midfield or sometimes as an extra midfielder-cum-striker, lying deep off a sole striker.

I know some football pundits felt that I should have left Swansea much earlier in my career to play at a higher level. I never regret the fact that I stayed with the Swans, as I felt loyalty was important, and I didn't want to let my colleagues or the fans down. This was an important factor, but I also thought that we were building something special, and I wanted to be a part of it. I still had the experience of representing my country more than 30 times, and I played both with and against some great players in those games.

When I'm asked to recall the best footballers I faced, two names immediately spring to mind: 'Der Kaiser', Franz Beckenbauer, who was a player with great class and composure, and the Soviet captain Oleg Blokhin, who could, when the mood took him, take teams apart by himself. The late 1970s and early '80s was also a time when the domestic game was laden with quality players, and I particularly rated the Scotland and Liverpool pairing of Graeme Souness and Kenny Dalglish. Probably the classiest British player I played against was Liam Brady, a really quality footballer who I remember swapping shirts with after he had given a master class in midfield play in a friendly at the Vetch.

Wales also had some great players. I've already referred to the striking qualities of Mark Hughes and Ian Rush, but I also thought that Kevin Ratcliffe of Everton was a highly underrated defender with excellent pace and great judgement. However, I would say the best Wales player I played with during my international career was Neville Southall. I played two seasons with Peter Shilton at the Dell, and he was a world-class keeper, but I still think that in a head-to-head I would have picked 'Big Nev' in my team.

I have very fond memories of my time with the international squad, although we didn't always experience the five-star treatment that John Toshack lambasted the modern Wales squad for taking for granted after the disastrous defeat to Cyprus in the 2007 Euro qualifying phase. Every year at the start of the Home International Championship, we were given one training shirt, one pair of shorts and one pair of socks, which were to last for the two weeks we were together. In May, it could be really hot or really wet, and after a few sessions my kit could walk to training whether I was in it or not. As our coach pulled up at Bisham Abbey before one game at Wembley, the England youth team were heading out to train, and every one of them looked immaculate in their brand-new training shirts and shorts. We all looked at each other, with our different-coloured tops covered in mud stains. Some of us were also wearing odd socks, and nobody would leave the coach until the youngsters were out of sight.

When I reflect on my Wales career, I am proud of what I achieved but more so for my family than myself. It was only after I finished with Wales that I realised just how proud my dad had been of me. I enjoyed every aspect of my international career, but I wouldn't be human if I didn't sometimes recall the period with frustration. Who knows what might have been if the Red Dragons had been given the rub of the green in some key games?

11

REFLECTIONS

As I was a professional footballer for over 20 years, it was always going to take me time to adjust to not playing any more. Being a pro is a unique job, and I naturally missed the banter and everyday comradeship. It also took time for me to adjust to the realities of having to organise my daily routine, as the clubs I'd played for had taken care of most of the day-to-day practicalities of my life since I was 18.

In recent years, there seems to have been a raft of autobiographies in which ex-players have talked about how they have gone off the rails after retiring and have failed to cope once their playing careers have finished. I would be reluctant to comment on these individual cases, but for me there was never any danger of this happening, despite going through the trauma of a separation and divorce from Pauline in the late 1990s. Although I missed the game, I knew I had been fortunate to have had a good career and to have played for my country, and I was fully prepared to embrace whatever the future had in store for me. I had made a good living from football, although I was far from rich, as the maximum I earned during my career was £500 a week at Swansea, which meant that I was never going to be able to retire at the age of 36.

CURT

Even though I hoped to continue in the game in some capacity, in the first few years after I retired I worked in different jobs, most notably for Abbey Life insurance company, and during my 18 months out of the game between 2004–05 I was a rep for the Hurns Brewing Company and a salesman for Bergoni for a few months. However, I never got a job offer from the Post Office, where many ex-Swans players worked, which was probably a good thing, as it would have been quite embarrassing not making their football team. The Swansea region won the British Post Office Cup several times in that period thanks to their ex-Swans contingent.

The people I worked with were very supportive and friendly, but I can't say that these were my dream jobs. I had been brought up to work hard, so I always worked to the best of my abilities. Although the last 15 years have not been without their ups and downs, I always remember my parents' advice that I should take the good with the bad, take every day as it comes and make the most of life.

My parents were the most important and influential people in my life, never mind my career, and I idolised both of them. My mother's death at such a comparatively young age had a massive impact upon me and was a real shock, as I thought she was indestructible. My father's death in 1998 was also very sudden, and there's not a day that goes by when I don't think about them. I will always be grateful for all the love and time they gave to me and Phil. Dad was my biggest fan, and I knew that he was always very proud of my achievements, but he also knew the game. If he thought I wasn't doing something properly, he would soon tell me. As for Mam, well, she simply thought I was the best player in the world.

As well as my mam and dad, I was also lucky to have Uncle Roy as a role model and positive influence on me. Even though he was a legend in the Valleys, Roy always made time for me, and his advice helped immensely when I was struggling to establish myself as a professional. I was really proud that Roy Paul was my uncle, and I always put him on a pedestal. I was very embarrassed early in my career when journalists would mention my name in the same breath as his.

I still have a copy of Roy's autobiography, which was published in 1956. Sadly, a lot of his memorabilia was lost when floods hit his home in Smith Street in Gelli, although his daughter Christine still has his medals, which she cherishes. I have kept some of my own memorabilia but have also given away a lot to friends, family and various charities.

Since retiring, the most special person in my life has been Clare, and I was delighted and honoured when in the summer of 2008 she agreed to be my wife. Clare is a very special woman, and we have a wonderful although often hectic life together. She is very patient and understanding, especially as my Wales job means that I can be away from home a lot and there is a lot of weekend work with the Swans. It can be very demanding on her, as she also runs her own business, Jabberwocky, a clothes shop in the Mumbles. We are very fortunate to have a great social life and spend a lot of time visiting or going out with our close circle of friends and family.

Clare and I especially look forward to the summer holidays when we can enjoy a week or two in each other's company without the distractions of our normally whirlwind lives. Holidays are a mixed blessing, though, because they also mean that we have to leave behind our gorgeous black Labrador Meg, who I am totally besotted with. Meg is great company, and after being let go by the Swans in April 2004 she was a great distraction for me. I hate being away from her for too long.

My family life is very important to me, and I have a good relationship with my ex-wife Pauline because of the bond we have over our sons. I am very close to and proud of my two boys: Ian, who is 30, and Gareth, who is 29. Ian is currently living in Canada and works in the restaurant trade, whilst his fiancée Clare is a qualified accountant. They plan to return home soon to settle down and get married.

Ian is the eccentric one in our family, and his choice of clothes is only matched by his changing hair colour. He has been blond, white, brown, black and, on one occasion, even purple. He has changed his hair colour so much that I'm not really sure now what it was to begin with!

Gareth works for the pension service but has always maintained that he is the real footballing talent in the Curtis family and that he would have made it all the way if it wasn't for his dodgy knees. Then again, he has said that he would have been a Hollywood star by now if the talent scouts had seen his performances in the school plays he appeared in. After school, he took a degree in software engineering and was awarded the 'student most likely to make you laugh' at his graduation, which I think is great and sums him up. Both Gareth and Ian are really great lads and get on well together, and they have often played in the same team for Mumbles Rangers.

Since meeting Clare, I have also got very close to her two lads, David and William, who are a real credit to their mum. Mind you, it's a good job we get on so well, as they have both been living with us rent free for the last few years. David is studying medicine at Bristol University, and William is at Cardiff doing dentistry. All four lads get on really well, although there are often heated debates as to who is the cleverest family – seems simple to me!

I had only been out of the game for about 16 months when I was offered the football in the community officer post at the Vetch, the scheme that was set up in September 1991, and I have been fortunate enough to be involved in football more or less continually since. In 1994, I had an offer from Frank Burrows to take a more formal role in a coaching capacity with the youth set-up. I found that I really enjoyed working with the youngsters and was really chuffed when we won the Welsh Youth League.

After Frank left the club in 1995, after four years of consolidating the club's position in the third tier of league football, the Swans had a revolving-door policy of managerial appointments. Between August

1995 and October 1997, the team had five managers: Bobby Smith, Kevin Cullis, Jimmy Rimmer, Jan Molby and Mickey Adams, who only lasted three games in charge. When Alan Cork became manager in October 1997, he offered me the position of first-team coach. However, the season proved to be a tough one, and even though we just avoided relegation Alan was sacked and replaced by John Hollins.

John was obviously a big name in the game, having had an outstanding career as a classy midfielder with Chelsea, QPR and Arsenal, and I thought that he might bring in his own men. Therefore, when he asked me to be his assistant manager, I couldn't have been more excited and accepted his offer. Under John's management, we won promotion to the Nationwide Division Two as champions in 1999–2000 in his second season in charge, and it really looked as if we could kick on from there. Unfortunately, there was a lack of money to invest – not uncharacteristic of the Swans in my experience – and we had to sell some of our better players. When we were immediately relegated back to the Nationwide Division Three, as it was at that time, John was sadly sacked. I was also dismissed as assistant manager, and Colin Addison took over briefly. However, I was reappointed to the same post by Nick Cusack before being reunited with my old friend Brian Flynn when he took over the helm in September 2002, alongside his close friend Kevin Reeves.

Of course, Brian and I were old friends, having played together for Wales for many years, and he had also been a great help to me when I moved to Leeds in 1979. I knew I would work well with him, which proved to be a good thing, as we struggled near the bottom of the division for the next two seasons.

A home fixture against Hull on 3 May 2003 stands out in particular from this period. In fact, after the club had left the Vetch for their new home at the Liberty Stadium in 2005, many fans voted this match the most memorable at the old ground. For non-

Swans fans, it might seem a strange choice, but before the game against Hull we were only one point ahead of Exeter, who had a better goal difference than us, and we were in real danger of losing our league status. Being so close to the abyss seemed to really unite the club and fans, and I think the sheer determination not to let Swansea drop out of the Football League was felt by everyone in the crowd that day. As first-team coach, I had to be calm in front of the players before the game, but my stomach was in knots as I thought about the possibility that my beloved Swans would no longer be a league club.

Throughout my career, I was never really one for ranting and raving in the dressing-room and was always one of the quieter team members. However, on that occasion I felt that I had to say something and try to make my contribution to what was a crucial moment in the history of the club. I think all my tension came out, and I talked about what the Swans meant to me and the fans, and how much responsibility the players had on their shoulders. I talked about the history of the club and how the 1958 Wales team had contained six Swansea-born players. I talked about Roger Freestone, our goalkeeper and longest-serving player, deserving to enjoy his testimonial season with the Swans as a league club. But most importantly I talked about the late Swans and Wales player Brian Evans, father of our physio Richard. A few weeks earlier, Brian had prayed on his deathbed that the Swans would stay up. I would like to think it was my Churchillian moment and helped inspire the players to a 4–2 victory, which kept us in the league, although local lad James Thomas, who scored a hat-trick that included a stunning 30-yard lob over Northern Ireland goalkeeper Alan Fettis, might also have played a small part in it.

Despite the stress and strain of being involved in the day-to-day running of a football club, I enjoyed the experience of being assistant manager under John and Brian. Apart from training the players, I also had to act as a buffer between the players and manager at times. My aim was to deal with any issues the players had before they escalated and reached the manager, and I'd like to think I was quite successful in this. As an assistant manager or coach, it is also important to share a footballing philosophy with the manager, and thankfully this was the case with both John and Brian.

The season after our traumatic brush with non-league football, Brian rallied the troops and results were much improved. It was, therefore, very disappointing when he was sacked, despite the team being in the top ten. Once again, I knew that my position at the club was likely to change. What I didn't envisage is how abruptly and with what little regard I was to be treated by the new Swans manager Kenny Jackett. I was very hurt, angry and annoyed when Jackett released me, mainly because of the abrupt manner in which it was done. It was all over in less than two minutes, and while it is always the new manager's right to make changes I felt that after over thirty years' service at the club it should have been handled better. I was quite sad at the time, because I really thought that my professional association with the club had ended. I didn't for one moment imagine that within a few years I'd be back working for the Swans again in a coaching capacity.

After nearly 18 months out of the game, Brian Flynn asked me to help out after he had been appointed head of youth development by John Toshack. Brian's brief was to develop Wales at Under-21, Under-19 and Under-17 levels, identifying and developing young Welsh talent. It was decided that two coaches, or intermediate team assistants, ideally one based in South Wales and one in the north, would help him out on a part-time basis, and I was delighted when Brian asked Joey Jones and me to take up the posts. Unfortunately, for various reasons, Joey was unable to accept the offer, so Dave Williams took over instead and has done a great job.

The Wales Under-21 team has often been seen as more of an inconvenience than a benefit to Welsh football and once went three seasons without a victory. However, under John and Brian the significance of youth football in Wales has been dramatically increased, and it has been a privilege to be involved in the development of some very talented youngsters. In recent years, the Under-21s have acted as a conveyor belt to the senior team, with, amongst others, Aaron Ramsey, Joe Ledley, Ched Evans, Chris Gunter, Gareth Bale, Wayne Hennessey, Jack Collinson and Sam Vokes making the step up, and I am sure that others, including Shaun MacDonald and Joe Allen, will soon follow them. With such a talented group of youngsters, the future of Welsh international football looks promising, and I think our chances of qualifying for a major tournament for the first time in 50 years are good.

It is my opinion that many of these players should have already played in a major tournament, as I can't ever recall a team winning their qualifying group, as we did for the European Under-21 tournament in Sweden in 2008, and then having to enter a play-off. We had a feeling as soon as we found out there was going to be a play-off that we would draw one of the major powers, and this proved to be the case when we were pitted against tournament favourites England. In fairness, we put up a fantastic effort and were maybe a little unlucky to lose 5–4 on aggregate. We were very proud of the lads, and I think we can continue to challenge at this level over the next few years, hopefully nurturing some more talent for the senior team.

I thoroughly enjoy working with Wales but was over the moon when Roberto Martínez asked me to return to Swansea in the autumn of 2007. Some people might think it strange that I would return to work for the club after the way I was treated in 2004. To my mind, however, individual managers and players move on but what really makes a club are its tradition, history and fans. Even though I have twice been sold by the Swans, and twice been sacked as assistant manager and head of youth development, I've always said I am attached to the club by a rubber band. I keep bouncing back and joke that the Swans can never quite shake me off.

My current role with the club is hugely enjoyable, and I am grateful that Roberto gave me the opportunity. My remit is to coach a group of the club's youngsters in the 18–20 age group in order to develop their technical skills. I agree with Roberto's emphasis on the importance of improving the players' basic footballing abilities, as foreign players generally seem to be more comfortable on the ball. Saying that, players such as Steven Gerrard and Wayne Rooney are admired worldwide and are able to combine great technique with a ferocious will to win.

My own philosophy is that although competition is inevitable in any form of football, development of young players is far more important than results. I try to make my sessions as enjoyable and varied as I can for the players so that they look forward to training. Coaching youngsters is a big responsibility, and sessions must be allowed to flow rather than continually stopped to make minor adjustments. It is essential that a coach keep talking to and encouraging his young charges. My best advice to young players is to repeat the old adage that those who fail to prepare should prepare to fail. Although I have managed players at first-team, reserve and youth level, my preference is being able to see the professional progression of younger players.

Having been a manager, I have great admiration for those who put themselves in the firing line on a daily basis, especially in these days of intense media scrutiny and fan pressure. That's why I particularly admire Manchester United's Alex Ferguson, whose success is unparalleled. I also think that Martin O'Neill has done a very good job at Leicester, Celtic and Villa and wonder whether my old club Leeds would have suffered the decline they have if he had replaced David O'Leary as manager in 2002.

If you are talking about good young managers today, you need look no further than Roberto Martínez, sadly no longer at Swansea. I'm sure he will be equally sensational at his new club Wigan as he was with the Swans. He is tactically excellent and very switched on. He obviously concentrates on his own team's strengths but is also able to dissect the opposition and therefore expose their weaknesses. He gives a lot of responsibility to his players, and in return he expects them to live and act like professional sportsmen, both on and off the field. Even though I have been in the game a long time, I picked up new ideas about coaching on an almost daily basis. Roberto's training programme, run in conjunction with Graham Jones, Colin Pascoe and Richard Evans, amazed me with its quality and variation. I would have loved to have been a player under their guidance, which is the biggest compliment I can pay them.

Saying that, however, I was lucky that I played under some very good managers during my career. In terms of man-management, I think the best managers were Lawrie McMenemy and Frank Burrows, who were both great motivators and who inspired great respect in their players. But I think Tosh was the best manager I played for, quite simply because he managed me during the best times of my career. He was tactically spot on and gave everybody confidence and a licence to go out and perform. He encouraged players to take risks and was especially good with forwards. Everything was simplified on and off the field, which meant that we could concentrate on training and playing. I think Tosh's recent achievements with Wales are often underestimated, and when he leaves the post he will leave the international team with a squad of players that will challenge for qualification for major tournaments for many years to come.

Fans often ask me about the main differences between playing today and in the 1970s and '80s. Comparisons with the past can sometimes turn into the standard 'It was much better in my day', with ex-players arguing that footballers today are paid more, better protected by referees and play on bowling-green pitches with featherweight balls. I'm sure that players from the 1950s and '60s could make the same comparisons between when I played and the conditions they experienced. What I would say is that there is a huge difference in the standard of medical treatment available today than when I was playing. In the 1970s, an operation on a serious knee injury would have about a 50 per cent chance of saving a player's career, whilst with today's laser treatment players having the same operations are often back training and playing within four to six weeks.

My main memory of treatment for injuries in the old days was the 'Magic Sponge', which could be very effective in encouraging a quick recovery. On freezing-cold and wet nights, playing up north in a midweek game, the sight, feel and smell of an icy sponge cured many an injury, I can tell you!

I think the other major difference between today and when I played is squad rotation, as it basically didn't exist back then. The manager picked his strongest team for every game. If you were in the team, you tried to stay there, whatever the fixture or competition. This often meant that you played carrying some niggling injury and not entirely fit.

During the four decades that I have been involved in football, the professional game has therefore moved on massively. However, one thing that I think remains constant is that football always produces outstanding players whom the crowds are happy to pay their money to watch. I have talked quite a bit in this book about the great players I have played with and against, and also those whom I have seen up close in my coaching capacity with both Swansea and Wales. If I was to pick a team from my own playing days, my Alan Curtis XI would be: Neville Southall in goals; Paul Madeley, Ante Rajković, Kevin Ratcliffe and Jimmy Hadžiabdić in the back four; Eddie Gray, Robbie James, Tony Currie and yours truly (well, it is my team after all) in midfield; Ian Rush and Mark Hughes up front; and Leighton James, Joey Jones and Jimmy Case on the bench.

I'm sure every player looks back on his career and thinks of what might have been. Certainly, I regret not qualifying for a major tournament with Wales, although representing my country was a great source of pride. The most difficult periods in my domestic career were spent at Leeds and Southampton. I don't regret my transfer to either club, but my time at both could probably be summed up with one word: frustration. A career-threatening injury ruined my time at Leeds, and my days at Southampton were littered with niggling injuries and personal tragedies. Although I had to think hard about signing for Cardiff initially, my time there turned out to be highly enjoyable under a great manager in Frank Burrows. I was happy to have played a part in a promotion-winning side, and to win over the fans and be voted Player of the Year gave me great personal satisfaction.

However, my playing and coaching careers will always be defined by my time with the Swans. I have loved every minute I have spent here and feel so proud to have played a part in a truly great era in the club's history. The rise from the bottom of Division Four to the top of Division One was a fantastic journey and an incredible experience for players and fans.

My association with the club has been a roller-coaster ride, and, to be honest, there have probably been more lows than highs over the years. However, the Swans are in a good position again, with a great stadium and an exciting squad of players. The loss of Roberto Martínez was a bitter pill to swallow for me personally, as I'm sure it was for the players and the fans. I felt that under Roberto's management the club was on the brink of something very special. I know that he agonised over his decision, but Wigan had a big emotional pull for him, as of course did the Swans. I can relate to his dilemma in making such a difficult decision, as I made a similar one myself when I left for Leeds in 1979. I just hope that the fans are as understanding of Roberto's decision as they were of mine and can remember the fantastic service he gave the club.

I get recognised quite a lot in Swansea and the wider South Wales area, and people often stop to chat about the past or the current state of Welsh football. I hope that this is partly because I gave people some pleasure when they saw me play, although it is really for other people to judge my abilities and my contribution to the game. I scored about 120 league goals, but I probably should have scored a few more if I am honest. I was once described as not being a great goal scorer but a scorer of great goals. I was always proud of that comment and am happy if that is to be the epitaph for my career. I have been privileged to have been involved in the game for so long and to have had such an eventful and rewarding career. However, I hope that my football story is not yet finished and that the future will bring more success, both with Swansea and with Wales.